# Bringing
# New Products
# to Market

# Bringing
# New Products
# to Market

*The Art and Science
of Creating Winners*

## John A. Hall

American Management Association

This publication is designed to provide accurate and authoritative
information in regard to the subject matter covered. It is sold with the
understanding that the publisher is not engaged in rendering legal,
accounting, or other professional service. If legal advice or other expert
assistance is required, the services of a competent professional person
should be sought.

Library of Congress Cataloging-in-Publication Data

Hall, John A. (John Alan), 1932-
    Bringing new products to market : the art and science of creating
winners / John A. Hall.
       p.      cm.
    Includes bibliographical references and index.
    ISBN 0-8144-5017-2 (hard cover)
    1. New products.  I. Title.  658.575
HF5415.153.H36   1991            HAL
658.5'75—dc20                    8.92                90-56188
                                                     CIP

Printing number

10 9 8 7 6 5 4 3 2 1

This book is dedicated
with love and affection
to
**Gwen Hall**
The student who has become the teacher

# Contents

Contents

## Section IV: Planning for New Products in Different Kinds of Companies     147

# Foreword

A first book, especially one in a subject area that already has a number of excellent books, deserves some explanation.

Nearly all the previously published works on new products concentrate on two relatively narrow segments of this truly panoramic subject: (1) the product planning needs and problems of the large, sophisticated, multiproduct companies and/or (2) the formulas necessary for giving birth to new products in the traditional Fortune 500 company, formulas that are inevitably designed for the bureaucratic, hierarchical form of corporate organization that is becoming increasingly obsolete in this second great age of the entrepreneur.

This book, in contrast, discusses the differences in product planning in various sizes and types of companies. In it, I offer specific suggestions to the entrepreneur and the growing company, as well as to the large corporation. Moreover, the "bite size" chapters not only permit the reader to focus sharply on specific product planning issues and the key interfaces of product planning with other company activities and functions, but provide ready reference for readers with specific information needs. Most important, this approach facilitates the kind of "short-interval reading" favored by many busy executives, who must read on the run.

I have oriented much of the material in this book to the information needs of the large majority of companies that are not in the Fortune 500 group. However, large and sophisticated companies will also find much value in this book, since I talk straight about some serious issues (such as the pernicious influence of politics on the new product planning process) that are glossed over in the more theoretical and academic tomes on new product planning.

I also hope to introduce this book to MBA students and college business majors. It can serve as a real-world supplement to basic texts on marketing, market research, business planning, and new product planning.

*Bringing New Products to Market* is based on my twenty-plus years of experience as a practicing management consultant and corporate planning and marketing executive. The book is written on two levels. On one, it describes key issues of concern to all who are directly involved in the new product development process—scientists, researchers, marketing and sales executives, and senior managers. From this perspective, *Bringing New Products to Market* can be classed as a professional book to be thoroughly read, referenced, and retained for future use.

On another level, I have attempted to make the treatment of this material light, readable, entertaining, and broadly informative. The mini-histories, for example, present in very telescoped form the key reasons why many major products, and some you may have never heard of, either made it big or bombed in the marketplace. The majority of these mini-histories derive from my professional management consulting and market research practice or from personal experience.

A minority flow from the application of market analysis to everyday products that the reader will relate to. Perrier, Coke, and Pringles, for example, fall into this category.

For the more casual reader, *Bringing New Products to Market* can be fully digested on a New York-to-California plane trip, allowing for dinner and a brief nap.

Many people have helped to form the attitudes, experiences, and the body of management practice I have attempted to encapsulate and compress into this book. Mac Rainie and the late Bob Montgomery were teachers and guides during my years at Stewart Dougall & Associates. Frank Leonard, president of Crossley Surveys, has been a continuing friend and colleague. Dick DeLuca guided me through the mysteries of the New York Stock Exchange.

My years at Pioneer Electronic Corp. enabled me to participate in the Japanese planning and management process in a way and at a level not available to many Americans. The late Bernie Mitchell, president of U.S. Pioneer, and the late Yozo Ishizuka, president of Pioneer Electronic Corp. of Japan, were teacher and role model, respectively. Pete Pryor, attorney for Pioneer, served as mentor and friend during those exciting years.

Several colleagues, clients, and friends have provided input and analysis on the mini-histories. Jerry Orenstein, Bob Donnelly, Tom Jones, Dennis Moran, Anand Kumar, Dick Lopez, Pat Janssen, Seymour Leichman, and Chuck Laverty have all made contributions that I want to recognize. Special thanks go to our colleague George Seiler, who provided mini-histories from his management consulting practice, which is oriented to chemical process industries.

My wife, Gwen E. Hall, who is a working product planner in the financial services field and who balances her roles as mother, wife, executive, and best friend with grace and wisdom, has been a continuing source of support, inspiration, and constructive suggestions.

The mistakes, omissions, and lapses, of which there must be some, are of my own making. Ironically, they will go largely unnoticed if *Bringing New Products to Market* is classed as a "Loser" in the game of new product introductions. If, however, it attains at least the status of "Modest Winner," the mistakes, lapses, and omissions will be public for all to see.

Special thanks to Jayne Swiney, Terry Isabella, and especially Sandy Robertson for their tireless work in retyping the endless changes in the text. And thanks to my staff at John Hall & Company, Susan Chmielewski, Mariola Obryk, and Mike Bernstein, whose diligence and professionalism enabled me to free up time to work on this book.

And finally, a word of thanks to my editor, Adrienne Hickey of AMACOM.

Although this book deals with the planning and marketing of new products, this is a first-time adventure in applying the disciplines described herein to the process of getting a book ready for publication.

Adrienne has guided me through this process with a mixture of courtesy, patience, and sharply focused professionalism.

# Author's Note

I have researched various available sources to ensure the accuracy and completeness of the information contained in this book. I have also drawn on information of a nonconfidential nature that I have had access to in the course of various employments and client assignments.

Any inaccuracies are unintentional and apologized for in advance.

## Product Liability Disclaimer

Readers or purchasers of this book are hereby warned that if they are purchasing or reading this book to discover the one sure process, system, formula, or set of rules and procedures that, if slavishly followed, will guarantee success every time in bringing new products to market, they will surely be disappointed.

After twenty years of involvement with new products, the one thing I can say with certainty is "There ain't no one magic formula."

I do claim, however, that if you will invest the approximately three hours required to digest this book, you will find at least several—and hopefully many—actionable ideas and insights that, if applied to your company, should:

- Improve your batting average
- Reduce your strikeout ratio
- Help you to win more frequently at the game of "bringing new products to market"

# SECTION I

# THE ROLE AND IMPORTANCE OF NEW PRODUCTS

New products bring many benefits to consumers as well as to the companies that bring them to market.

In this section, the benefits brought by new products are analyzed. The various kinds of new products are also defined.

I also identify and discuss new product success and failure rates and the reasons why so many new product concepts abort and why so many new product introductions fail in the marketplace.

# CHAPTER ONE

# Why New Products Are So Important

New products are the lifeblood of American business. They are drivers of progress and serve as milestones by which we all measure the enrichment of our lives and the progress that we are making in fulfilling our human wants and needs.

Successful new products are often the cornerstone on which great new companies—and, indeed, new industries—are built. The first electronic computer, the first xerographic process copier, and the first motion picture are examples of new products that have been the foundations of new industries, each of which has created hundreds of thousands of well-paid jobs.

Successful new products bring many benefits to the companies that introduce them, apart from the benefits they provide to the customers who use them. Companies that are consistently successful in bringing new products and services to market find that they achieve some or all of the following benefits from their new product introductions:

1. *New products create excitement, build commitment, and make a company a more exciting place to work.* We live in an age when worker commitment, and especially the commitment of the well-educated, the inner-directed, the innovative, and the

entrepreneurial, no longer automatically attaches to the current employer. A company that consistently generates exciting new products will have a greater opportunity to hire and retain these valuable people than one that does not generate successful new products.

2. *New products enable companies and salespeople to strengthen existing customer relationships and to build new ones.* At every one of the thousands of trade shows held every year in the Free World, the customers, the media, and the competition all gravitate to the booths of the companies with exciting new products. Old customers who have fallen away to competitors return to the fold, and representatives, agents, and distributors scramble to represent the line and the product. Doors that have been closed to your salespeople for years are suddenly opened, and trade reporters who previously never mentioned your company line up to interview your key executives.

3. *The pull-through effect of important new products on your whole line is often significant, and almost always underrated.* In the current business environment, the short-term bottom line is almighty, and financial people often make the critical go/no-go decisions on new products. Financial managers often have elaborate models, formulas, and company statistics to help them make the go/no-go decision. But rarely do they make any serious attempt to quantify or properly value the extra sales and the incremental profit on their established products, which they receive from the pull-through effect of the successful new product.

This is perhaps the single most important failing of financial management relative to new products. Financial managers are often very precise, as they should be in calculating the total cost of a new product launch. They analyze and program such factors as direct factory costs, new equipment needs, advertising and promotion costs, breakeven rates, cash flow, and return on investment (ROI). But rarely is there a serious effort to quantify or measure these side benefits, which should be factored into the new product go/no-go decision.

4. *New products provide an excellent opportunity to reposition*

*the company to the various key publics that it serves.* Each of the publics with whom the company has relations and with whom it communicates—employees, customers, competitors, suppliers, government, and investors—has an interest in new products. A successful new product—or better, a proven track record in continually bringing successful new products to market—permits the company to restate its message and to reinvigorate its communication with each of these publics. Again, financial managers usually give little or no weight to this factor when go/no-go decisions are made on new products.

5. *In almost every industry, a steady stream of successful new products is essential to avoid decline and to fuel continued growth.* Old products decline, and their sales volume and their profit erode. Growth in the size of the market is often outside your control. Growth in market share for established products is often expensive to achieve. Competitors match or copy your established products, often at lower prices.

In new products, as in every other area of business, there are numerous 80/20 rules. My close involvement in new products over a twenty-year period has persuaded me that new products have very significant energizing and synergizing effects. New products are often responsible, directly or indirectly, for a large portion of the incremental profit enjoyed by growing companies.

# CHAPTER TWO

# What Is a New Product, Anyway?

I recently saw a segment of *60 Minutes* in which Andy Rooney poked fun at a number of well-established products for using the words *new* or *improved* on their packages or in their advertising. This reaction is not atypical. It reflects the current confusion over the question, "Just what constitutes a new product, anyway?" (see Figure 2-1).

## The Five Categories of New Products

After more than two decades of research, analysis, and planning related to bringing new products to market, I have concluded that 99 percent of all new products and services can be usefully classified into one of five categories: (1) the breakthrough product, (2) the "it's new for us" product, (3) the new, improved, next-generation product, (4) the line extension product, and (5) the 3 *R*s.

### The Breakthrough Product

Breakthrough products are what most people have in mind when they think of new products. They include the first

**Figure 2-1.** The five categories of new products.

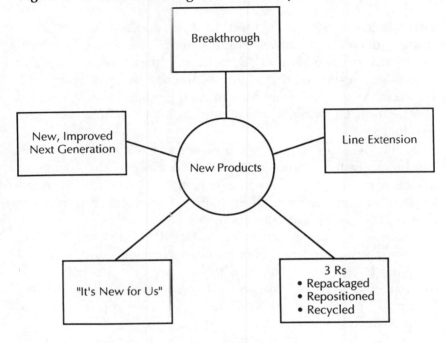

personal computer, fax machine, and videocassette recorder. But they are also the first *Baseball Encyclopedia*, the Donvier Ice Cream Maker, the first diet sodas made with aspartame. They are the countless "new" new products that result when a new technology or a new approach to an old need has been realized into a specific product or service that is demonstrably different from, and hopefully better than, the product it replaces.

I will discuss many breakthrough products in this book, but a company that wants to be successful in bringing new products to market cannot depend wholly or even primarily on such products. There are four other categories of new products, each very important in its own right, that together account for a very large majority of the sales and profits derived by most companies from new products.

## The "It's New for Us" Product

Often a company finds itself in a position where it must design, make, and market for the first time a product that is already on the market. Sometimes this move is a defensive one, designed to retain a market or a segment of business. Often the company finds it necessary to meet the competition by bringing out a replica of the innovator's new product.

The decision to make a product already on the market can be motivated by the desire to "get a piece of the action" in a high-growth market, but more often it is based on the need to gain market share or additional sales by adding a product that has already gained acceptance in the market.

Consider and analyze very carefully your reasons for devoting valuable R&D and product development effort to bringing to market an "it's new for us" product that is not new to your customers or prospects. The question, "What do you bring to the party?" should be rigorously applied to any planned introduction in this category.

Seriously probe this question in your product planning strategy sessions. If you and your key advisors can't come up with one or more real benefits that you would bring to the party (e.g., lower cost, higher quality, meet unfilled demand, superior marketing, better service), you may be best advised to pass on this "it's new for us" product and focus on more creative and profitable approaches.

Some excellent companies (e.g., Matsushita Electric) have built huge and profitable businesses primarily by making established products cheaper and better, and by marketing them more aggressively than the company that introduced the breakthrough product. But all too many of the companies that rely heavily upon the "it's new for us" approach are branded as dull, me-too, follower companies by their customers and by the financial community. The fruits of following this policy, to the exclusion of all other approaches, are often low market share, high employee turnover, low morale, below-normal profits, and a constant struggle merely to stay alive as a company.

## The New, Improved, Next-Generation Product

With all due respect to Andy Rooney, I would argue that there is indeed a legitimate category of new, improved, next-generation products. To qualify as such, a product must have one or more of the following values, features, or improvements that were not available in the last-generation product:

- A new chemical, ingredient, flavor, feature, or benefit, that in some way makes the product taste better, work better, act faster, or fill some need, real or psychic, not filled by the previous-generation product
- A reduction in the cost of the product or an increase in the durability or the working life of the product
- An enhancement of the functional design that makes the product easier to use, set up, or install—computers being a good example here

In short, the new, improved, next-generation product must add some value factor not present in the last-generation product. The overwhelming majority of new products that make the new and improved claim have a legitimate right to do so. The few that do not inevitably fail in the marketplace.

## The Line Extension Product

Line extension products probably represent the most straight-forward, often mundane, approach to bringing new products to market; but it is an approach that is usually profitable.

Line extension products include the following:

- The large economy size
- The small take-along-in-your-travel-kit size
- The upgrade model
- The step-down model
- The full-featured model
- The no-frills model
- The new package, bottle, can, plastic container, and others

Line extension products are responsive to the specific needs and life-styles of important segments of your market. While not as exciting as breakthrough products, they demonstrate to your customers, your salespeople, and your employees that yours is a market-driven company that listens to its customers and makes a real attempt to be responsive to their needs.

Here I must warn against the oversegmentation and proliferation of trivial differences that often pass for sophisticated product planning in mature, low-growth markets. Beer, cigarettes, detergents, and a host of other consumer package goods have often taken the concepts of market segmentation and new product differentiation to ridiculous extremes. The announcement and subsequent withdrawal of Uptown, a cigarette positioned toward black consumers, is an example of this tendency to oversegment markets and proliferate unnecessary product entries.

## The 3 *R*s

The 3 *R*s are *r*epackaging, *r*epositioning, and *r*ecycling.

1. *The repackaged product.* Even if the basic product is unchanged, a new package can supply a freshness and vitality that allows you to resell to established customers and to sell to prospective customers who have resisted your product to date.

A new package design can often give new life and vitality to a product in the eyes of both current customers and potential new customers. Giving a product a new name is often a highly effective variant of repackaging.

I talk later in more detail about the naming of new products. Here I will simply say that the new name must be well publicized and promoted. A decision to introduce a new name should be made for specific strategic reasons based on research in the marketplace. The change from Datsun to Nissan cost tens of millions of dollars to implement and was not accomplished without some *agita* on the part of the dealers who market these excellent cars. All this effort and expense has proved very worthwhile.

2. *The repositioned product.* The strategic positioning of a new product is a subject worthy of a book in itself. I consider *Positioning, The Battle for Your Mind,* by Reis and Trout (New York: Warner Books, 1981) to be the classic work on this subject.

In the context of my work, I recognize the strategic repositioning of a product against a new market or to meet a new need as a legitimate form of bringing new products to market.

One example is Church and Dwight, whose Arm & Hammer Baking Soda had been a staple in American kitchens for years. Church and Dwight repositioned Arm & Hammer Baking Soda as a "breath freshener" for products stored in the refrigerator. The result was a dramatic increase in sales for what had been a stable, mature product.

3. *The recycled product.* On occasion, a product that has been bypassed by new technological developments can be recycled or remarketed for a particular purpose. Some years ago, ceiling fans were largely replaced by air-conditioners and were thought by many to be an obsolete product, used only by the poor who could not afford air-conditioning.

In recent years, the ceiling fan has been recycled as a fashion product, with a wide variety of styles and colors to coordinate with modern or Victorian styles of home decoration. The product category has had a strong renaissance, partly as an energy-saver, but mostly as a style and fashion accessory.

The fountain pen, once the writing instrument of choice, was overwhelmed by the ballpoint pen and more recently by the felt tip pen. Waterman, once the dominant fountain pen supplier, has survived by marketing beautifully designed, upscale, and expensive fountain pens to be used as a badge of distinction by senior executives and others.

The breeding and raising of horses was an important

occupation as late as the 1920s, filling the needs of basic transportation and of the cavalry. Horse breeding and horse raising survives today as a much smaller business but a sharply focused (and sometimes very profitable) business filling the need for racehorses to entertain the masses and for show horses to gratify the super-affluent.

# CHAPTER THREE

# New Products—Who's in Charge?

The question "Who's in charge?" is important in every area of business. The question takes on special importance for the new product development process and the management and coordination of all the steps that must be accomplished in the process of bringing new products to market (see Figure 3-1).

Ultimately, of course, the company owner or president is responsible for the new product generation and marketing process. However, in nearly all Fortune 500 companies and in many smaller companies, the president must delegate the management and coordination of this activity to someone else or, more commonly, to a formal or informal product planning/product development committee or task force.

One of the reasons so many small entrepreneurial companies are consistently able to beat their larger, better-financed competitors to the market with new products is the close involvement of the entrepreneur in the new product planning and development process. The "hands on" entrepreneurial chief executive officer (CEO) is often personally involved in designing, inventing, or manufacturing the new product. He or she knows the critical path and personally cuts through problems to speed up the product development cycle.

The CEO of the large, complex company must necessarily

**Figure 3-1.** Roles of key people and functions in bringing a new product to market.

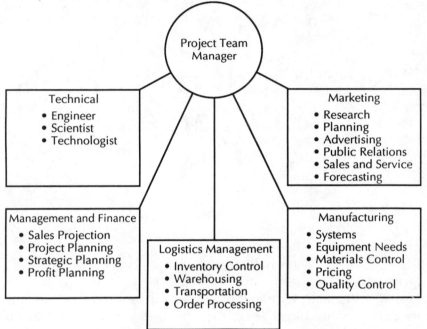

delegate this responsibility. Often, for political reasons, but sometimes for legitimate reasons of control, balance, or morale, the CEO of the big company opts for a task force or planning committee approach to bringing new products to market, rather than putting one person in charge of the whole process. Some large, complex companies, such as International Business Machines Corp. (IBM), Hewlett-Packard, and 3M, have mastered the fine art of remaining responsive to market needs while involving many people and departments in a complex, interdependent process of planning and generating new products.

However, for every large, complex company that has worked out an efficient, responsive product planning committee/ task force approach to new products, there are many more that suffer from inefficient, bureaucratic, highly politicized product planning committees or task forces. In such companies, the appointment of one senior executive, with close access to the president, and with full authority over all of the elements involved in bringing new products to market, is a better answer.

A team builder, a person who can relate well to engineers, scientists, marketers, salespeople, and manufacturers, is the person best suited to head the new product development process.

Critical to the success of this activity is the development of a corporate culture that is highly supportive of the new product development process. I say more about this in Chapter Eight. Here, suffice it to say that organization should follow function. The element of the new product planning process (R&D, product development, marketing, manufacturing, and so on) that is most critical to the success of the new product in your company is the area that should have final responsibility for new product planning.

The decision of who is to be in charge of new products is not to be made lightly. There is no one formula answer that is right for all companies, or even for one major industry group.

Here are four recommendations that may be helpful regarding all the activities necessary for bringing new products to market successfully.

1. A person, not a committee, should be in charge. That person must have both the personal leadership qualities and the mandate from top management to make decisions and to move things along.
2. Success at all levels should be well rewarded. In large, public companies, rewards should approach those enjoyed by entrepreneurs.
3. Failures should be examined very fairly and intensively, and specific steps must be taken to see that the same type of failure does not become a pattern. Remediation, not scapegoating, is the proper attitude for dealing with the problem of "why did we goof on this new product?"

4. The person in charge should be able to mold people from different departments, different disciplines, and often different styles of working and communicating into a harmonious, effective, and supportive new product project team.

# CHAPTER FOUR

# Success and Failure Rates With New Products

The consulting firm of Booz, Allen & Hamilton, Inc. has done exhaustive research on the success and failure rates of new products. Their research indicates that, of the new product concepts generated through product planning processes, on which R&D and product planning time and money are expended, only about 15 percent ever make it to the market as new products.

Among those products that do make it to the market about 65 percent, or two of three, are judged to be successful. But there are many degrees of "success," and this two-of-three figure includes many line extension products and new, improved, next-generation products whose "success," meaning they were not withdrawn from the market, is virtually guaranteed but often of a limited nature.

My own personal experience with new products is consistent with the 15 percent birthing rate for new concepts and the 65 percent success rate for the new products that do get through the process and make it to the market. But, for breakthrough products and for new products marketed by many small, entrepreneurial or start-up companies, the success rate is much lower than 65 percent.

The questions, then, in analyzing the process of bringing new products to market are:

1. Why do so many products fail?
2. What can be done to increase a company's success rate in bringing new products to market, both in reducing the failure rate of new product concepts and in increasing the success rate of the products that do make it to the marketplace?

Our answers to the first question can be found in Chapter Five. Answers to the second will be found throughout the balance of the book.

# CHAPTER FIVE

# Why So Many New Products Fail

In our practice, we have identified seven primary causes that account for about 95 percent of the reasons why new products fail (see Figure 5-1).

## A Bad Idea With a Powerful Product Champion

The powerful, dynamic CEO of an entrepreneurial company can often become enamored of a product idea that, for one or many reasons, is not going to fly in the marketplace. Often, the market is too small or specialized, the product will cost more than the market will pay for it, or the market is not ready for the product. But the powerful product champion can ignore facts, refuse to do market research, and often bully or cajole his or her subordinates into going forward and investing time and money into a bad product idea.

## The Solution in Search of a Problem

In technology-driven industries and companies it is often possible and usually necessary to generate exciting new technologies that really do represent excellent technological breakthroughs. However, when technical people are given the

**Figure 5-1.** Sources of new product failure.

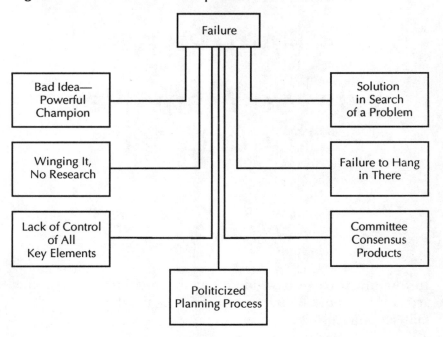

full power to plan new products, they often concentrate on perfecting new technologies rather than on developing specific products to meet current or future needs of customers. The result is "the solution in search of a problem."

A classic case of this is videotext (see Mini-History 7, this section), a marvelous technological innovation for which American consumers in two major market tests decided that while the technology was great, the value of the service received was not worth paying for. Too many alternate, less costly options that provide this same information were already widely available.

## Winging It—Going to Market With Little or No Good Market Research

No market research, or poorly planned or poorly executed market research, is a major cause of new product failure.

Many entrepreneurs pride themselves on being so "close to the customer" that they believe they don't need to do any market research on new products.

On the other hand, many professional product planning people who have ample budgets for market research too often conduct unimaginative "cookie-cutter" market research that fails to get good answers to the really important questions:

- Who, very specifically, is going to buy this product?
- What are the specific reasons or motivations why they will buy it?
- What value does the new product provide that is not now available on the market?
- How much money are potential customers willing to pay for it, at most?
- What is the message or "hook" that must be used to get the attention of prime prospects so that they can be converted to customers?

## A Highly Politicized, Revolving Door–Type Product Planning System

Often top management is totally preoccupied with making the next quarter's numbers or with spending most of its time with investment bankers either buying the stock, planning a take-over, or defending against one. When this happens, the folks back at the ranch are inclined to get restless. A direct result of such weak or noninvolved top management is often a product planning process that is used by ambitious product planners or marketers more to further their own ends than to design, develop, produce, and market superior new products that the market really needs or wants.

When top management fails to focus on new products, the process often lacks goals, thrust, urgency, and direction. Individuals pursue their own new product directions, coordination between departments is poor, memo writing proliferates, and good new product ideas are shot down or delayed by those who do not want to see their competitors for promotion gain an advantage with an exciting new product.

The use of the product planning department as a staging area where young, often inexperienced people are sent to find a horse to ride or to make their bones is all too often a fact of life in such companies.

Poorly planned products, hastily developed and sketchily researched, often result when "fast track" people are permitted to use the new product planning process as a vehicle for becoming line managers for the new products that they, or someone else, developed during their brief stay in the new product planning holding pen.

New product planning and the bringing of new products to market is a critical activity that should be entrusted to professionals skilled in the necessary disciplines of planning, research, and analysis and who identify their future with that of the company. Most important, they must relate to and have a feel for the products they are planning to bring to market. Any other approach is a recipe for failure.

## Failure to "Hang in There" for the Time It Takes a Good New Product to Become Established in the Marketplace

I am a firm believer in setting specific, quantifiable goals and targets for new products and time frames for achieving them. However, I also advocate contingency planning and the drafting of best case/worst case scenarios for new products. It is a fact of life that many new products, especially technically advanced breakthrough products, require a fairly extended period of market makeready or market development before they are accepted by your customers.

The concept of running a breakthrough product at a sizable loss for an extended period of time has been known to induce numerous cases of *agita* in financial executives and CEOs preoccupied with the "bottom line this quarter."

One of the major reasons that Japanese companies have become dominant in so many high-technology areas is that they understand far better than their American competitors the need to invest time, money, and marketing manpower in market development or market makeready for many breakthrough products.

## Not Having Control Over All Key Elements in the Process

Sometimes the planning of the new product depends on the development of a process, a key module, or part (or worse yet a new technology) by an outside vendor or a joint venture partner not under your control. This situation occurs frequently among small high-technology companies and is one of the great strengths and the same time weaknesses of the Silicon Valley electronics firms.

A small company with limited resources often finds it necessary to subcontract out one or more critical elements of a new product development project. Defense contractors do this as a matter of course. But they are not subject to the disciplines of the marketplace. Cost overruns and failure to meet new product development schedules are just passed on to the taxpayer.

But for small companies that are subject to the disciplines of the competitive free market, failure of subcontractors to perfect the process, module, part, or technology on time and on budget often leads to financial ruin for the project and sometimes for the company.

## Committee-Type Product Planning That Produces a Compromise or Consensus Product Rather Than a Sharply Focused Product

The consensus product planning process, in addition to being slow, cumbersome, and expensive, often leads to compromise products that are positioned to a broad middle market. Such products are often picked apart by competitors, who target specific features and benefits in their own new products to specific-niche markets. The all-purpose product designed by a committee to appeal to all segments of the market and to incorporate all the pet ideas of all the committee participants usually fails to excite buyers who have specialized needs. Again, this is one of the reasons entrepreneurs thrive while large companies working with infinitely more time, money, and resources so often fail in their new product planning efforts.

Most of the remaining 5 percent of new product failures can be attributed to the thousand and one management mistakes or "goof-ups" that plague us all. These include:

- Poor pricing (too low or too high)
- Poor quality control (excessive returns and ultimately customer rejection)
- Poor timing of the product introduction
- Lack of support from salespeople, sales representatives, or retailers

# CHAPTER SIX

# Sorting Out the Losers Quickly and Easily

In Chapter Four I noted that 85 percent of the concepts generated for new products fail to make it to the market. Most companies can dramatically improve on this high failure rate if they will follow certain basic rules relative to generating and evaluating concepts for new products.

## The Obvious Bad Ideas

One way to reduce the new product concept fail rate is not to restrict or inhibit the concept generation process but rather to screen out the obviously bad ideas *very early in the process*, with minimal time and expense wasted on them.

Many obvious bad ideas that make it into the product planning process either come from people who are not close to the customer or who have no concept of the relative cost/benefit ratios of the products.

A new product idea should not be automatically discarded if it doesn't come from a star salesperson or key customer. But the level of knowledge and sophistication of the person who submits the idea should be a factor in how much time and effort are allocated to that particular new product idea, at least initially.

Most obvious bad ideas exhibit one or more of the following characteristics when subjected to rigorous analysis:

- They test very poorly when the concept is shown to a small number of highly knowledgeable potential purchasers. As noted, focus groups or one-on-one meetings with key customers can often expose a bad idea quickly and inexpensively.
- The highest price that potential customers will pay for the product is considerably below the "first-pass" estimated manufacturing costs.
- The new product does not really address any clearly perceived need in the marketplace.
- The product has strong appeal only to a very small segment of the market, or—more deadly yet—the product has only a low level of appeal to a broad spectrum of the market. The former is the product that is so specialized, so exotic, and usually so expensive that only a very small segment of the market would have any interest in purchasing it; too small a niche for the product to be viable. The latter is the classic "stuck in the middle" product.

## The Not-So-Obvious Bad Ideas

Products that are too new and too different from current products and usually require a market makeready period should be suspect, especially if the company is not willing to commit the resources of time, people power, and money to conduct the necessary market development.

New product concepts usually have a less than average chance of success if the following conditions are present:

- *There is pressure from top management to get a major new product fast.* Unfortunately, this scenario often occurs in companies that are in financial trouble precisely because they have not had a strong new product planning culture all along.
- *The technology needed to make the concept work is still under*

*development.* This is the archenemy of the small high-technology company that is straining to use the leverage of a breakthrough technical product to gain competitive advantage against larger rivals.

- *The product is a breakthrough product in an area with which the company has limited experience.* A very dangerous kind of

**Figure 6-1.** Bad new product ideas and how to spot them.

| | |
|---|---|
| **Product already matured in market:** | • Calls on "due bills" from customers, reps to get sales<br>• Low profit margins<br>• Window of opportunity lost<br>• Often sells only on low price<br>• May not be profitable |
| **Pressure from important customer with untypical needs:** | • Customization of standard product<br>• Market research will show if need is widespread |
| **Panic and pressure for big new product soon:** | • Task forces and committees<br>• No product champion<br>• Unrealistic budgets and time frames |
| **Powerful person with a bad idea:** | • Suppression of reality<br>• Foot dragging<br>• Personnel turnover<br>• "Tailor" research to desired outcomes |
| **Consensus, compromise product not sharply focused to customer needs:** | • Vulnerable to competition<br>• Often must price below market<br>• High volume, low profit<br>• Misses key market segments |
| **Solution in search of a problem:** | • Provides features, not benefits<br>• Often costs more to produce than customer will pay<br>• Market often not ready to adapt to technology |

new product scenario. Some say Murphy's Law was invented to cover this situation.

• *The product is an "it's new for us" product that is already matured in the marketplace.* Thousands of companies get caught up in this scenario. Often this occurs because your product launch date has slipped out, while at the same time the market for the product has matured and peaked faster than had been expected.

• *There is pressure from an important customer whose needs are not typical of the needs of the overall market.* This is a special challenge for manufacturers of industrial products or producers' goods.* Sometimes it is necessary to talk with key customers and to reach an alternative solution to their needs that will be less costly for all concerned.

Figure 6-1 summarizes the evidences and results of bad new product ideas.

*Producers' goods are products sold to other companies that use them to make, fabricate, or produce other products (e.g., printing presses, machine tools, industrial robots).

# Mini-Histories

# 1

## The American Express Credit Card

### Investing in the Infrastructure for Long-Term Success

It may be hard for people under age 35 to accept, but there really was a time when there were no plastic credit cards. In 1951, a small, unknown company called Diners Club introduced the first credit card. This created a small sensation and the company was, for the first several years, very successful.

But a breakthrough product, especially a very successful one, always brings competitors. In this case, the American Express Company, very large, very successful, and very cash rich, zeroed in on this new credit card business as an ideal new business to build on its strengths as America's number-one financial services company for the traveler.

American Express launched its own credit card in the late 1950s after an intensive study of the potential market. While many times larger and financially stronger than Diners Club, American Express recognized that it must make significant investments in advertising, promotion, and operational systems to dislodge Diners Club from the number-one position in this emerging market.

By a strange quirk of fate, I was associated with two firms that made crucial contributions to the successful launch of the American Express credit card during the critical startup period.

Reuben H. Donnelly Corporation, which markets the Yellow Pages for New York Telephone and other Bell System Companies, was retained to sign up every major restaurant and many retail establishments for a free Yellow Pages trademark listing, if the establishment would agree to honor the American Express Card. This campaign met with almost total success in Manhattan thanks to the efforts of six management trainees who "hit the bricks" during a humid July to accomplish this signup.

One year later I was employed as a systems analyst and sales trainee for a business forms printing and design firm. This company was heavily involved in designing the internal systems and controls and the resultant business forms that were needed to provide the infrastructure to support the rapid growth of the American Express credit card business.

By the early to mid-1960s, American Express had taken market leadership away from Diners Club. To this day, despite vigorous marketing efforts on the part of MasterCard and especially Visa, the American Express credit card is still considered by many the preeminent credit card worldwide. As of early 1990, 33 million American Express cards are honored at 2.7 million establishments in 130 countries.

The breakthrough product, the Diners Club card, limps along with a small market share. The follower American Express, because it invested early on in the upfront marketing, the building of a solid base of loyal retailers, and most important, invested in the systems design and people needed to support its growth, has taken and held the mantle of leadership in this market for over two decades. For these reasons, American Express was rewarded in its credit card market introduction with a Big Winner.

In Chapter One I noted that some major new products can create a whole new industry. Indeed credit cards, or "plastic," are both an industry, quite profitable and fiercely competitive, as well as a life-style for millions of people.

## Key Lesson

American Express recognized the need to make significant upfront investments in building a strong base of American Express retailers as well as a strong systems support infrastructure. This kind of investment can be critical when you are trying to launch a major new service business.

# 2

## The Swatch Watch

### It Comes in Color
### Everywhere

The Bulova Watch Company was one of the mainstays of the watch industry when the Swiss ruled the world of watches. The advent of the quartz watch and the rise of K. Hattori Corporation and its Seiko brand to dominance forced Bulova to a strategic redirection of its business.

The company's first reaction was to concentrate on the upscale market, watches with elegant styling retailing for $100 or more. However, this upscale market accounts for only about 10 percent of the watch volume.

Some serious product planning and smart research convinced the Bulova management to strike out in a new direction to regain its share of market. This new strategic direction was to look at watches as fashion merchandise and to design a line of colorful, imaginative, kicky, and youthful watches to be priced to compete with the low end of Seiko and the mainstream of Timex watches. The product was named the Swatch Watch, which serves as a perfect illustration of the power that an imaginative name has in helping to establish a new product in the market.

Bulova positioned this watch as fun fashion at a low price against the youth market. In fact, older people, recognizing that the Swatch Watches were the smart thing to wear, soon started sporting them in place of their Rolexes and Caravelles. The concept of a Swatch Watch to match each of the key outfits in your wardrobe was skillfully developed by Bulova in a print media advertising program. Because it had the willingness to see an old product in a new light and was able to shift its focus from Swiss craftsmanship to American high-style fashion, Bulova has created a Big Winner with the Swatch Watch.

## Key Lesson

When your basic expertise in an industry becomes eclipsed by new technology, you have a serious problem. Sometimes the correct strategy for dealing with that problem is to reposition the product from a basis of engineering or high quality and reliability to more of a fashion-oriented one. The creative approach taken by Bulova helped it to resolve a difficult problem. By repositioning and repackaging the watch and marketing it as fashion goods, Bulova created a new market segment that has expanded the watch market.

# 3

# RCA Capacitance Videodisc Player

## The Bad Idea With a Powerful Champion

In Chapter Five, I identify the "bad idea with a powerful product champion" as one of the principal reasons why new products fail in the marketplace. The RCA capacitance videodisc player, on which RCA took a write-off of over $400 million in 1984, is a classic illustration of this truth.

In the late 1970s, RCA brought to the market a videodisc player that was low-priced and had an excellent catalog of supporting programs. Moreover, the marketing plan was powerful, thorough, and professionally executed by the marketing and sales organizations of this powerful company. The product received an avalanche of publicity prior to its introduction. The introduction itself was a gala event, complete with press party, and with both the trade media and the Wall Street financial community in attendance. The initial sell-in of product to RCA accounts was accomplished very smoothly.

The only problem was that the capacitance video technology was a "needle in the grove" technology incapable of significant refinement or upgrading. In contrast, the laser technology of the optical videodisc was then in its infancy and capable of much refinement and upgrading over time.

The powerful champion behind the RCA capacitance videodisc player was none other than then-chairman Edgar Griffiths, according to several media sources. Griffiths was concerned that all recent new innovations and breakthrough products in consumer electronics were coming from Japan. Griffiths was determined to prove that American electronics technology was still competitive and still capable of developing a major new consumer electronics technology. His thesis may or may not be true, but the capacitance videodisc player was not the proper product on which to make that bet.

So, because the RCA organization was unwilling or unable to tell the boss that he was backing a bad idea, a fine sales and marketing organization worked brilliantly only to produce a Loser in the capacitance videodisc player. RCA took a loss announced at over $400 million when it discontinued sales of the capacitance videodisc player, and the company's stock price went up.

## Key Lesson

A new product planning system that fails to provide good feedback to top management from line sales managers, retailers, and consumers is a recipe for failure. Subordinates need to have the courage, self-confidence, and job security to tell the boss the real facts about a new product concept. A bad idea with a powerful patron is going to be a Loser in a large majority of cases. Spending lots of money on advertising and sales only adds to the loss.

# 4

## Pringles

## One Mo' Time—Why Pringles Didn't Make It!

Every book and every college course and seminar on new product development that I am aware of uses Pringles as an example of a new product introduction that was less than stunningly successful. At the risk of being judged redundant or presumptuous, and with all due respects to my colleagues and competitors, I present herewith my own analysis of the market introduction and the continuing saga of Pringles.

There are several reasons why Pringles has become a classic or staple in the repertory of the product planning pundits.

First, we all learned from the cradle through our MBA degrees that Procter & Gamble wrote the book on product planning, and that when Procter & Gamble does it, it does it right.

Second, Pringles was widely trumpeted as a triumph of product planning, package design, and marketing know-how in an industry (potato chips) that was regarded as unsophisticated, old-fashioned, and unprogressive.

But somehow those local, country boy potato chip makers have survived and prospered while Pringles, with its beautifully designed cans and neatly stacked chips, barely survives as a marginal player after fifteen years of brilliant product planning and marketing.

So what's the matter with Pringles? Well, first there's the name. Pringles is a great, cute name—for a singles bar in Manhattan or an agency for English nannies—but not, heaven help us, for a crunchy, meaty potato chip. Second, there's the little matter of taste and texture. Procter & Gamble assembled the finest team of package designers, food technologists, and product managers on earth to bring Pringles to market (Chapter Five notes that the "committee, consensus, compromise" product is a prime candidate for failure). To make uniform-sized and uniform-shaped chips that neatly stack in a cylindrical can, it was necessary to compromise and to use dried, reconstituted potatoes rather than raw, natural spuds. To concoct a potato chip able to compete in texture or crunchy taste with, say, Granny Goose or Wise, starting with dried reconstituted potatoes would be the gastronomical equivalent of squaring the circle.

Prior to writing up this mini-history, I tried afresh the three readily available flavors of Pringles: regular, BBQ, and onion/garlic. I submitted them to my very unscientific "How does the stuff taste?" test. All three varieties were significantly better than the original Pringles I once taste tested years ago. My compliments to the Procter & Gamble food technologists for their continuing efforts to square the circle.

But still, Pringles must be rated as a Loser, since the majority of consumers have refused to accept neatly stacked chips in a can as a substitute for the original potato chip made from raw spuds—warts, bumps, and all.

## Key Lesson

If a new product idea has a major intrinsic flaw or limitation, then all the creative marketing, product planning, and financial resources you can muster may not be enough to permit a full success in the marketplace.

# 5

## Guaranteed Ice

### Upgrade From a Commodity Status by Providing What the Customer Really Wants

Basic Leasing Company leases equipment—ice machines, dishwashers, commercial ovens—to restaurants and bars in the greater New York City metropolitan area. Its many competitors market and sell mostly on the basis of financing advantages, balance sheet improvement, and ease of obtaining the equipment.

Basic Leasing is different. Its managers asked themselves and their target customers what it was these customers wanted and needed in order to operate. They identified that a clear requirement for restaurants and bars was to have ice available whenever they need it, twenty-four hours a day, seven days a week. No ice, no drinks: No drinks, no profits.

Basic Leasing ensures that its customers are *never* without ice. It leases ice machines with the guaranteed availability of ice. If for any reason whatever an ice machine is not producing, Basic Leasing delivers ice to the customer while the machine is being repaired. This is of real value to customers, ensuring that their bars and restaurants will never be without ice, a key ingredient to their profitable operations. It allows them to solve such a problem with a single phone call.

This added service repositioned Basic Leasing's product of leased ice machines and changed the whole nature of the market. This service is what differentiates Basic Leasing's business from that of other leasing companies. Although ice delivery to any single location is very expensive, because Basic Leasing spreads the cost of this service across all of its leases, the company is able to charge a reasonable fee and make an attractive profit. And along with the ice machines, some customers also lease other equipment from Basic Leasing because it is convenient to do so.

Is "guaranteed ice" a new product? Indeed it is. Although the physical things Basic Leasing does are fairly standard, the features and benefits are new and have a major favorable impact on customers. No worries about being out of ice and no need to have alternative supply arrangements in place. A simple solution is provided to what can be a major problem with only a modest, known cost increase to customers for this comfort and assurance—and *no surprises.*

This is a superior-niche market new product and at least a Modest Winner in the marketplace.

## Key Lesson

The role of the supplier is to identify and satisfy what the customer really wants and needs; when this occurs, there is real value added, and customers will pay up for real value added.

The best way to consider a customer's objectives may be from a systems point of view—not just product and not just service, but the in-use product and service combination.

Basic Leasing Company repositioned a mundane commodity product into a product/service package by adding a new value, the guarantee of ice at all times.

*—George Seiler*

# 6

# L'eggs

## Nothing Beats a Great Pair of Marketing Ideas

Women made the transition from wearing nylon stockings to pantyhose in the late 1950s and early 1960s. However, pantyhose quickly became commodity-type products with little brand differentiation and with purchases being made on the basis of convenience and price. Hanes, one of the leading makers of pantyhose, attempted to develop a new upgraded positioning for the product that would establish the company as the dominant supplier.

A new strategy was developed that was extensively tested through market research and test markets. The basic concept revolved around a unique new packaging concept whereby the pantyhose was housed in egg-shaped boxes, and the name L'eggs was coined.

Research confirmed that the retail marketplace was very open to selling a proprietary branded product with a unique positioning as opposed to a low-margin undifferentiated commodity product. Most important, because of its packaging, L'eggs was positioned to sell in grocery and drugstores, greatly facilitating the impulse purchase of pantyhose by working women.

Hanes also launched and has maintained a major advertising program to support L'eggs. This product quickly became the dominant brand in the pantyhose business. A quarter-century later the product's unique packaging remains as popular as ever with the public and Hanes is still the dominant company in the pantyhose business.

Surely a Big Winner in every respect, L'eggs exemplifies the power of a unique name combined with memorable packaging even for a commodity product.

## Key Lesson

If you have one strong marketing idea, such as the unique packaging design of L'eggs, you have a high likelihood of success. Your prospects for success grow geometrically if you also have a brilliant name for the product and an imaginative new approach to the channels of distribution to be employed.

# 7

# Videotext

## I Think It's Great, But Let Someone Else Pay For It

In the late 1970s and early 1980s, the concept of videotext was thought by many to be the next major revolution wrought by the magic of consumer electronics.

Videotext systems provide a wealth of data and information from such mundane items as train and plane schedules, weather, and stock prices to vast storehouses of information on almost any conceivable subject. All these data could be readily available on your TV screen following a telephone call or better yet, by calling up information via a keyboard touch pad or touch screen.

England, France, and West Germany had all developed sophisticated videotext systems using various technologies and approaches.

Two major American test markets of the consumer reaction to videotext were conducted, one in Florida by the Knight Ridder newspaper organization in combination with American Telephone and Telegraph (AT&T), the second by CBS and Time, Inc., in Ridgewood, New Jersey. Considerable resources of time, people, and money with attendant media publicity were devoted to these videotext test markets.

The results of the two tests were conclusive and depressingly similar. The upscale, affluent consumers in these test markets gave very high approval rates to the videotext systems but were strongly resistant to paying hard money for these services. They equated the service with free TV and thought that sponsors who had an interest in one or more of the services highlighted by videotext should pick up the costs of the system rather than the user. In truth, most of the information provided by videotext was available free from other sources or was of such marginal value or such specialized usage that it was not possible to convince people to pay the basic charge for the service.

We suspect that at some point in the future, videotext will become a staple fixture in the American home, but as of the early 1980s it was a classic illustration of the "solution in search of a problem," which happens when techies, not businesspeople, make the marketing and planning decisions. A major breakthrough product, the videotext concept must at this time be classified with the Losers.

## Key Lesson

When technology is pursued for its own sake, the consumer will still be the ultimate arbiter on the new product. Even when a bad idea gets through the planning process, disaster can still be averted by well-planned test markets. Certainly it was cheaper for the companies involved to find out the consumer reaction to videotext in test markets than after a costly national introduction (see Chapter Nineteen).

# 8

## McDonald's Japan

### Adapting a Winning Formula to a Different Culture

The growth of McDonald's from a six-store chain in southern California to an American institution employing more people than General Motors has been well chronicled. A similar success story has been achieved by McDonald's in Japan thanks to the efforts of a singular entrepreneur, Den Fujita, who adopted the McDonald's formula to the unique situation of Japan.

The story, as told to me by Fujita and recounted in his biography, reveals much about the character of the Japanese people, Fujita himself and McDonald's. Ray Kroc, the late president of McDonald's, chose Den Fujita as his Japanese partner in 1971. Fujita, already a successful importer, recognized that due to the xenophobia and other traits of the Japanese, some creative adaptations of the successful McDonald's formula would be necessary to establish the business in Japan. First, because of Japanese pronunciation the name would be spelled and pronounced Mak Udo Narudo. After much discussion, this was accepted by Ray Kroc.

Second, it would be necessary to open the first McDonald's not only in Tokyo but in the heart of the Ginza.

Third, the target market would be the critical fifteen- to twenty-year-old age group.

Most important, McDonald's would be positioned as a Japanese fast food chain, not as an import from America. Also hamburgers were to be introduced not as a food but as a cultural product. Since beef and french fries were not eaten widely in Japan at that time, McDonald's was introducing a new element into Japanese culture or life-style. Great emphasis was placed on providing the usual excellent Japanese

courtesy to all customers and to surpassing even the high
levels of training, management, oversight, and cleanliness set
by McDonald's USA.

By 1990, there were over 500 McDonald's in Japan, and
Den Fujita rightly claims to be the largest importer of Western
beef and Idaho potatoes in the world. The combination of
Japanese expertise and the McDonald's formula was an instant
Big Winner that gets bigger every year. McDonald's Japan, a
billion-dollar company, is now the largest restaurant chain in
Japan.

## Key Lesson

A successful franchise operation provides a proven formula
for running a business. And no franchise operation in the
United States has been more consistently successful than
McDonald's. However, the entrepreneur who brought McDonald's to Japan had the wisdom to realize that he must fine-tune
the success formula to his own unique market. Den Fujita
repackaged and repositioned the McDonald's formula to fit
the unique character of the Japanese market to ensure a
successful introduction of beef and potatoes to people who for
a thousand years have lived on fish and rice.

## Winning Ideas

1. New products are the lifeblood of business. Their importance extends far beyond revenue contribution to a firm's profit and loss (P&L).
2. Every new product idea should be characterized by type. This exercise will aid in evaluating your product's near and longer-term potential.
3. It is usually better for one person rather than a committee to have overall authority for new products. That individual should be long on people skills, a professional adept at team building, not a technician.
4. Only about 15 percent of the new product ideas actually reach the market. About 65 percent of the new products introduced to the market are judged successful. Both the 15 percent birthing rate and the 65 percent success rate can be substantially improved by those who pay sufficient attention to their new product.
5. There are seven major reasons that account for 95 percent or more of new product failures. They are all easy to spot, if you look for them, and most can be avoided by companies that are really committed to succeeding at bringing their new products to market.

# SECTION II

# STRATEGIC PLANNING FOR NEW PRODUCTS

This section looks at new products from the perspective of the strategic planning that must be accomplished if you are to be successful in bringing the new product to market.

I deal here with the relationships and linkages of new products to:

- The business plan
- Corporate culture
- The company profit and loss statement
- The sales forecast
- Pricing strategy
- Advertising strategy

Failure to interface the new product introduction with these activities often results in a poorly planned, poorly executed, and suboptimal new product introduction. Conversely, if all of these activities are thoroughly considered and factored into the rollout plan for the new product, the chance for a truly successful product launch is much enhanced.

# CHAPTER SEVEN

# Role of New Products in the Strategic Plan

Every company preparing to introduce a new product should develop a long-term strategic product plan as a key element of its strategic business plan. The plan must address four basic questions:

1. Who is our customer?
2. What does the customer buy?
3. What is "value" to the customer?
4. How can we gain competitive advantage?

This plan will provide guidance to the technology planning people and product planning people in terms of the general guidelines for new product development that the company will follow.

This strategic product plan should consider at least the following specific issues:

1. *Should we attempt to secure a new product leadership position in the markets we serve, or will we accept the role of a cost-efficient, market-responsive close follower?* Each strategy has its merits and demerits, and the correct answer varies from company to company. Product leadership works best when the lead time

for your competitors to copy you is lengthy and when being first allows you to corner a large market share. For small-niche products, a posture of product leadership is often essential.

But for small companies that lack strong financing, a posture of being a close follower reduces the risks of being blown out of business by the failure of a breakthrough product.

2. *What specific kinds of products or new product opportunities are to be sought out by the product development people? And which ones are to be avoided?* Product planners need to be in close touch with your customers' perceptions of the strengths and weaknesses of the company. If your perceived strength is a certain technical expertise or a particular quality feature, new products that play to these strong suits are what you should be on the lookout for.

New products that build on your base of technology or expertise, or that sell to the same customer or market segment where you already have a strong position, are likely to be winners. New products that require convincing your customers that you really have the know-how or expertise required are less likely to be successful in the marketplace.

3. *Are we going to attempt to be the low-cost producer of the industry?* Usually the posture of being the low-cost producer only works when two or more of the following conditions obtain:

- You have the highest market share.
- Your labor or raw material costs are significantly lower than those of competition.
- You have newer, more efficient production machinery and/or production techniques than do your competitors.
- Low price per se, rather than a competitive price with other value features added, is the key to success. This usually occurs in a commodity-type market where it is not possible to add value or to distinguish your product from that of your competitors.

4. *Will we seek to maximize market share by aggressive new product development?* When new product leadership can be used

as a lever to get business on the existing product line, this indicates use of aggressive product development as your strategy for gaining market share dominance.

5. *What percentage of sales will be generated by new products?* Some companies, including many large and successful ones, set as a corporate goal a fixed percentage of sales and profits that will be generated by new products that were not in the product line three or four years ago. This kind of specific goal can serve to focus the attention of all concerned on the need to aggressively seek out, develop, and market new products as a continuing way of life.

6. *Will top management commit to a steady state product development effort even in years of reduced profits? And at what level of funding?* This is the acid test of whether the company truly has a strong culture of new product leadership. Even companies that are winners at producing a steady stream of new products in profit years will be tempted to cut back severely on new product development at the first sign of a sales or profit downturn.

But most Japanese companies and the best-managed of American companies resist the temptation to gut their new product development efforts to appease the wolves of Wall Street.

7. *How good is our competitive research, and do we have a good fix on what our competitors are planning relative to new products?* It is vital that the company monitor the new product development activities of key competitors. This kind of competitive intelligence must be factored into your own product planning strategy.

8. *How fast is the technology going to change, and how quickly are competitors going to introduce new products?* A good rule of thumb is that when new technology is being introduced at an accelerating pace, that pace will probably continue to accelerate.

It is critical that you make a realistic estimate of the time window that your breakthrough product will have before competition reaches the market. A worst-case scenario arises where you must invest an amount of time in market development and market missionary work that is approximately equal to the time it takes for your competitors to reach the market with their low-cost directly competing product.

## Integration With the Corporate Business Plan

It is critical that the entire process of bringing new products to market be organically linked to the business planning unit and to the corporate business plan.

The business plan should have one section specifically devoted to new products. This section should cover these two issues:

1. The importance of new products to the goals, objectives, and results of the company in the form of a strategy statement.
2. The role that new products will play in strengthening the strategic position (e.g., market share, profit) of the company in each major market or line of business.

A new product based on a proprietary technology or patented feature can help take business away from competitors and can help boost profit margins. The extent to which new products will be used to enter new markets, to open new customers, and to improve the overall competitive situation of the company needs to be evaluated and quantified in the business plan.

An analysis of the relative importance of *each* of the five kinds of new products [(1) breakthrough, (2) "it's new for us," (3) line extensions, (4) new, improved, next-generation, and (5) 3 *Rs*] in achieving specific goals of the company should be accomplished.

Depending upon your industry and its degree of maturity, different kinds of new products will have different kinds and degrees of importance. High-growth, high-technology markets place greater emphasis on breakthrough products and the new, improved, next-generation products.

Companies in mature, low-growth industries are more likely to look for line extension products along with new, improved, next-generation products.

# CHAPTER EIGHT

# Corporate Culture and the People Side of New Products

It should be obvious by now that a successful new product introduction is not the work of one person or even of one department. Companies that win consistently at new products are invariably those where bureaucracy, in-fighting, politics, and turf issues are subordinated to common goals and a common vision.

Indeed one motivation for writing this book was my conclusion that the currently available books on new products, which are excellent in many respects, do not place sufficient importance on the people side of new products. They emphasize process, which is certainly important, but the urgent need to carefully select the right people for the new product team and to get every department in the company to lend willing and enthusiastic support is critical. These issues need to be faced squarely and honestly.

The blunt fact is that all too many bureaucratic companies—and bureaucratic departments within companies—prefer to avoid the risks, struggles, uncertainties, and plain hard work associated with designing, making, and introducing major new products. The ways in which corporate bureaucrats can slow down, cast doubt on, or downright sabotage new products that would threaten their cozy status quo are legion; requests for more study, more financial analysis, and more review of the impact on next year's profits are only a few of the time-honored approaches bureaucrats utilize to give the "slows" to a new product that has the potential of upsetting existing power relationships.

Many American companies aggravate these tendencies by setting new product planning people apart, both physically and psychologically, from their co-workers. In the typical Japanese company and in the more advanced American companies, new product planners are physically located in the factory building, not in some remote and fancy research park. And Ph.D. scientists mingle easily with manufacturing foremen, ware-house managers, order entry clerks, and especially with cus-tomers. A feel for the company, a love for the product, and a passionate concern about serving the customer and improving the product/service mix—these ingredients are as essential to success as the academic and technical skills of the product planner.

It is imperative that the product planning people take a good temperature reading on the corporate culture as it affects new product development. Critical issues include the following:

- Do the culture of the company and the systems, controls, and priorities that exemplify and codify this culture encourage people to seek out breakthrough product and other new product ideas?
- Do the rewards for acting as product champion for a winning new product outweigh the potential risks of being associated with a losing new product?
- Are the various staff support people (e.g., advertising, legal, systems, personnel, logistics) whose assistance is needed at various points in the process ready and eager to lend their time and talents to new product projects? Or must they be dragged kicking and screaming to the product planning table?
- Does the new product planning system have sufficient

flexibility to afford special treatment for the potential major new breakthrough product?

The most important factor is the level of support and encouragement you receive from corporate headquarters, especially in large, complex companies. All too often, companies that manage quarter-to-quarter and measure their success only by price/earnings ratios, ROI, and similar financial indicators lack deep-down commitment to any new product effort that will, in the short run, adversely affect the balance sheet, the income statement, or the stock price. If this is the prevailing culture in your company, you have only three options:

1. Go along with the flow and concentrate on sure-thing, low-impact new product introductions. Go for singles, not home runs.
2. Strive mightily, cleverly, and persistently to change the corporate culture with regard to new products. This approach requires making alliances and endless hours of education, persuasion, and "politicking" in the good sense of the word. But be prepared for years of frustration and only partial success absent a major management change.
3. If your greatest expertise and satisfaction lies in new product development, rework your résumé, contact the executive recruiters, and relocate to a more fertile field in which to exercise your talents.

Sometimes external events can force a change in corporate culture. This has happened, for example, in the deregulated seven regional Bell operating companies (BOCs), which have a special need and a special challenge in bringing new products to market. After a century in which a powerful corporate culture that emphasized excellence in the area of service had become solidly entrenched, the rules were drastically changed. The reality of divestiture has forced the Bell system companies to become market focused and to compete with outside competitors and with each other in developing a wide range of new products and services.

AT&T itself has responded to this challenge with enthusiasm, with some good new products and with a major shift in its corporate culture. After several stops and starts, several massive layoffs, and some costly new product introductions, such as the Unix system computers, AT&T is now starting to develop a true marketing and new product planning culture, while retaining its service orientation.

The seven regional BOCs, which were expected by many analysts to have much greater problems adjusting to deregulation than AT&T, have actually outperformed their former parent in many respects relative to bringing new products to market. At both AT&T and the regional operating companies, a vigorous new product planning process is now well established. This process is actively supported by management at AT&T and at the BOCs.

If the century-old Bell System can establish a new product-oriented corporate culture, you can too!

# CHAPTER NINE

# New Products and the Product Manager

The product manager concept, which proved its worth over many years in consumer package goods marketing, has now been adopted by many companies, large and small, across a broad spectrum of industries.

The product manager typically has full profit and loss responsibility for the brand or product and calls on all the staff and line resources of the company to accomplish this task.

Traditionally, the product manager has been a specialist in his or her profession or art rather than a person who is deeply immersed in the technology and the dynamics of the specific product that is being managed.

Typically an MBA with a marketing major, the consumer package goods product manager is highly skilled in the techniques of merchandising, consumer market analysis, package design, advertising, and research. Relative to products, product managers are interchangeable parts who can move quickly and easily from toothpaste to macaroni to frozen TV dinners, without missing a beat.

Product management traditionally has been a fast-paced, high-intensity, high-turnover "burn out" business in all too many companies. In many consumer package goods companies product or brand management has been the quickest path to the executive suite.

However, when the product to be planned is a consumer durable, an electronics product, or a high-tech manufacturing product, a heavy dose of in-depth product knowledge and specific market experience is also essential to success.

As a company grows in size, complexity, and sophistication, the time will come when product management should be introduced to the company.

A question critical to the process of bringing new products to market is: At what point in the new product planning process is the product manager named and what are his or her responsibilities, relationships, and interfaces during the often long and complex product development process?

The companies that are most successful in making the transition to a product manager mode of organization are the ones who "grow their own" rather than hiring professional product managers from the consumer package goods marketing companies.

The choice of the right people to become product or brand managers is not made lightly. Direct sales experience is vital but so is the analytical mindset and a creative flair not often found together in the same person. Considerable people skills are also essential along with an easy facility for dealing with high-level corporate politics.

The roles and specific responsibilities of the product manager relative to other members of the marketing team must be spelled out in detail.

No one standard answer to this question fits all cases, but there are several situations that can be discussed with profit:

• *Only a major new product can afford or can justify the expense of a fully dedicated product manager during the planning stage.* Line extension products, new, improved, next-generation products, and most "it's new for us" products usually do not require a dedicated product manager. Breakthrough products, especially major ones, often require at least one full-time dedicated product manager.

The complexity of the new product introduction, the

expected level of competition, and the importance of the new product, both in terms of sales and the strategic position of the company, should be considered in making the decision to invest in a product manager.

- *The person best-qualified to be product manager, who will manage the introduction and guide the critical first years, often emerges from the product planning team.* This is often the person who becomes the product champion, who pushes the new product through the many stages of the bureaucratic new product approval process. Sometimes in a smaller company the product manager is the person who initiated the new product or who pushed for its inclusion in the line. Needless to say, the product manager must truly believe in the product and be totally committed to its success. This person must energize the sales force to give its best efforts to a successful launch.

- *The product manager may, in smaller companies, handle many products and may have a number of duties beyond product management.* It is essential, relative to breakthrough products, that this individual's duties and responsibilities be clearly defined on paper. This description needs to be clearly communicated to all members of the new product development team, as well as to senior management. As noted above, the breakthrough product often requires special handling and should not be put on the standard new product assembly line.

# CHAPTER TEN

# The New Product Sales Forecast and P&L Statement

One of the most critical issues in bringing new products to market is the sales forecast for the product. This should be made by quarter for the first year (or in some cases by month) and should be made on a yearly basis for five years or for the expected product life-cycle, if less than five years.

The sales forecast for the new product and the techniques for arriving at the sales forecast will vary, based on the category of new product.

When the new product is a new, improved next-generation product or a product-line extension, there is usually sufficient historical data to permit development of a fairly tight sales forecast.

Sales forecasting for breakthrough products and "it's new for us" products relies heavily on a combination of market research, expert judgment, and detailed analysis of the likely reaction of competitors.

As discussed later in this chapter, I also recommend a three-level forecast, one that brackets 90 to 95 percent of the possible range of outcomes, based on estimates of those closest to the product and your very best market research.

Very few companies do the kind of best-case/worst-case forecasting needed to execute proper contingency planning for the new product. A company should not proceed with the product introduction unless it is prepared to live, for some time, with the conservative scenario.

## Consumer Products

It is critical that the sales and profit results of the new product be closely monitored and frequently reported to top management. For products that are sold through retail channels of distribution (department stores, grocery or drug stores, or other specialty retailers), it is important to measure your company's sales (the sell-in), but it is absolutely vital to measure the sales by the retailer to the end consumer (the sell-through).

Many companies delude themselves into thinking a new product is a winner based on a strong initial sell-in of the product to the retail distribution chain. Based on this strong sell-in, they ramp up production and add new production capacity. To do this prior to the receipt of concrete evidence of a strong sell-through at retail is often a recipe for disaster.

Various tracking services and store audit services are available and can be readily used for this purpose. We often recommend the establishment of a small network of "barometer stores" (often about fifty), whose sales patterns, taken together, are predictive of the national pattern.

These barometer stores are provided with various incentives to give you accurate and timely feedback on who is buying and who is not buying the new product during those critical first weeks of market introduction.

Close, continuing follow-up by your salespeople, reps, or the marketing department on the barometer stores is essential to this strategy. For consumer products, you want to know who specifically is buying the product. You want to measure, to the extent possible with your limited resources, the relative importance of in-store displays, product demonstrations, dealer sales support, shelf positioning, and cents-off or other incentives in generating sell-through at retail.

## Industrial Products

For industrial goods companies or products and services sold directly to the end user, early sales should be tracked and analyzed sale-by-sale, account-by-account, and by segment of the market. You need to develop estimates of the hit rate (e.g., sales as a percent of quotations, number of calls necessary to achieve a sale). Most important, you need accurate, fast feedback on who is not buying and the reasons for nonpurchase. It is critical that salespeople provide real feedback direct from the customer, rather than their own surmise of why the customer didn't buy the product.

Watch closely for early patterns that indicate that one particular size of customer, one particular sales district, one particular end use application, or one particular industry is picking up on the product faster than others. Some of these patterns will be random and idiosyncratic, but some will tell you specifically where to focus your marketing manpower and your advertising dollars to generate the early momentum that will signal to the market that your new product is a Big Winner.

For the "complex sale" that involves a number of different people on the buy side (for example, purchasing, engineering, end users), it is vital that your sales organization touch all bases and monitor, expedite, and coordinate the sales process. Most important, you need to discern early in the process whether the key people at your prospective customer are really interested in the new product or are merely going through the motions to keep your salespeople happy.

The Japanese have perfected the art of "considering your proposal" ad infinitum as opposed to telling you your new product or your idea is a "bummer." Many sophisticated American companies have adopted this same approach to dealing with vendors.

Industrial products, especially producers' goods, often are driven by the needs of a major customer. In this case, it is important to determine if this customer's needs reflect those of the market at large. Otherwise, your new product may have very limited success.

## When Things Look Bad

If a new product is not making it, you need to know immediately whether you have a pricing problem, a product acceptance problem, an advertising problem, a selling problem, or whatever. If the problem can be quickly identified, remedial action can often be taken to salvage the product launch. In some cases, a quick kill of a new product idea that is obviously not making it is the right decision. In other cases, some fine-tuning of one or more elements in the product/pricing/marketing mix is the indicated strategy. For breakthrough products that aren't making their numbers, a stretchout and increased market development expense are sometimes the preferred solutions.

However, when the new product is obviously not making it, it is rare that to "just keep keeping on" with no strategic changes is the right solution to the problem.

## Budgeting for New Products

The budget setting process and the time frame set for product planning and R&D must be based on the realities of this unique set of activities.

The creative act of finding the right process or technology to solve a design problem or provide a performance feature by its very nature involves much trial and error. The legendary story of the invention of the incandescent lamp by Thomas Edison claims that he tried over 5,000 experiments before he found the right approach to bring this breakthrough product to reality. If Edison had been working for a large, bureaucratic corporation run by the numbers, perhaps we would all still be reading by gaslight.

Too often the same formulas used to prepare budgets for routine ongoing operations are applied to the R&D functions and new product development, often with unhappy results. This does not mean that senior management and financial controllers should abdicate their responsibilities in the special case of the breakthrough product. But the planning, scheduling, and management of this activity must come to terms with the reality that this new product birthing process is often bumpy, discontinuous, and agonizingly slow. The creative testing and translating of new ideas and new technologies into tangible products and services cannot be programmed with the same precision as, say, that of an up-and-running manufacturing facility.

## The Hurdle Rate of Return Fallacy

I am a strong advocate of developing detailed sales and expense budgets for new products and for close monitoring and timely reporting of actual results against these forecasts. I do not, however, subscribe to the "make numbers this quarter and everything will be fine" school of management.

Companies that operate in this mode—and despite their lofty mission statements to the contrary, there are thousands of them—often lack the patience to develop winning new products and the conviction to stay with them and promote them until they are successful.

For many years, conventional business planning dogma held that any new product must clear a "hurdle rate of return" before funds could be invested in its development, production, or marketing. The hurdle rate of return was defined as a level of profits that covered the interest cost on the funds to be invested in the new product *plus* a rate of profit that does not reduce the total profitability of the company.

Companies that followed the "hurdle rate of return" philosophy relative to new products typically avoided breakthrough new products and focused on safe but unspectacular new products.

Hopefully, the current movement toward a more entrepreneurial approach to management will consign the "hurdle rate of return" concept to the dustbin of business history.

The "hurdle rate of return" approach to judging new products almost always fails to give proper weight to improvements in competitive position resulting from successful new products. It also fails to consider incremental sales and profits that come from established products because of the pull-through effect of strong new products, especially breakthrough products.

I would argue that the financial standards and criteria that the company employs for new products should be different for different categories of new product.

The breakthrough product, if successful, can often dramatically improve the total position of the company. Therefore, the company should be willing to support breakthrough products and to sustain losses on them for some period of time if this is warranted by the long-term profit prospects.

A thorough analysis of both long-term sales and the long-term profit potential and competitive situation should be accomplished for every breakthrough product in the course of setting the financial plan for the product.

If the breakthrough product is likely to have a long product life cycle and if it is protected by proprietary technology or patents, if the entry cost of competitors is high and your overall financial position is strong, then you can properly take the long high road to solidly establishing the breakthrough product. Specifically, this means the following:

- Low, keep-out pricing
- A long, sustained market development or market make-ready period
- An advertising and marketing communications program that is soft sell and educational as opposed to hard sell and promotional
- A sales organization that takes time to thoroughly explain features, uses, applications, and benefits as opposed to one that pushes hard for orders right now

On the other hand, if your time window of exclusivity is short, your competitors strong, aggressive and well financed and your resources limited, you may be better advised to adopt a "take the money and run" approach to financial planning for the breakthrough product.

In-depth analysis of the dynamics of the product itself, the served market, and your current or likely competitors must be accomplished in both strategic and financial terms if you want to craft the right financial plan for your breakthrough product.

It is often advisable for the company to go forward with breakthrough products even under the following scenario.

| | |
|---|---|
| *Year I:* | Large out-of-pocket loss, no absorption of overhead |
| *Year II:* | Small loss or breakeven |
| *Year III:* | Losses in earlier years are recouped and product is now operating profitably |
| *Year IV:* | Product solidly profitable and established as a leader in the marketplace |

You should especially watch the line extension product for any signs of cannibalization. The line extension product should add true incremental sales, not merely substitute sales. Many companies fall into the trap of adding new line extension products that have the net effect of spreading a given amount of sales volume out over more line items with no increase in total sales. Line extension products that merely increase your manufacturing, distribution, and marketing costs will lower your bottom line profit and often serve no valid strategic purpose.

New, improved, next-generation products and line extension products, for which the market is already established, usually should be expected to pull their weight in terms of profit contribution, almost from day one.

"It's new for us" products are in many respects the most difficult for which to set reasonable and proper profit contribution goals. On the one hand, the company has many of the startup and learning curve problems normally associated with the breakthrough product. Yet the reaction of the market to your "it's new for us" product is often one of indifference or lack of excitement. Frequently, sales managers need to draw on their due bills from customers or use the overall strength of the product line to induce customers to switch from their established supplier to buy your "it's new for us" product.

If indeed the product is a straight copy of existing products and does not offer any special benefit, feature, or value not already availa)e, it may mean that price competition is your only viable market entry strategy. This approach has worked very well for Korean and Taiwanese manufacturers who were competing against Japanese suppliers in a wide range of products, such as clothing, consumer electronics, and automobiles, where they enjoyed a very considerable labor cost advantage. Absent such a competitive edge, the "it's new for us" product that brings nothing special to the customer is often destined either to fail in the marketplace or to provide sales volume only, with minimal or even negative profit contribution.

Close involvement of budget planners in understanding the dynamics of new product introductions is essential. An appreciation of "how the numbers work" for various kinds of new products in various market situations is necessary. Hands-on product planning people can usually supply this kind of input to the budget department, on the basis of their experience in the market.

It's important to prepare a three-level projection (optimistic, expected, conservative) that brackets 90 to 95 percent of the range of possible outcomes for sales in units and dollars. Marketing expenses and profit contributions must be stressed.

When there is a three-level plan, all the key people in Finance, Marketing Manufacturing, and top management can visually plot and monitor the progress of the new product much more easily than if the standard one-case plan is used. Now that nearly everyone has access to a personal computer and basic spreadsheet programs, each person on the team can readily monitor progress against the three-case projection on his or her own microcomputer.

I cannot stress too often or too urgently the need for collegial and cooperative rather than adversarial relationships between the people on the one side who plan, design, make, and market the new products and those on the other side who create budgets, draft business plans, dictate investment decisions, and otherwise handle financial matters.

Far too many "MBA finance types" approach new product planning and market introduction meetings girded for combat. They see their role as one of protecting the profit plan, the ROI, and the return on assets record against the incursions of those "sales and marketing types" who want to spend those precious, hard-won profit dollars on risky, untested new product ideas.

The new product people for their part must accept the need for tight cost control, PERT charts, GANTT charts, and other such planning disciplines, which finance/planning people routinely utilize.

A whole school of management literature in fact and fiction has pitted the "right brain" creative entrepreneur against the "left brain" orderly planners and controllers. The great companies, the successful companies, know that you need both to win at the game of new products. And the two hemispheres must work together as part of one team.

When realistic sales and expense budgets are set for new products and agreed on prior to launch, much unnecessary tension and adversarial posturing is removed from the process. Financial people can then support and explain the P&L projections of the new product during management reviews.

# CHAPTER ELEVEN

# Pricing Strategies for New Products

One of the most important questions that must be dealt with in bringing new products to market is pricing. (See also Chapter Twenty-Two on pricing research for a further discussion of this subject.)

Price theory states that a breakthrough product, if its unique values are recognized and fill a genuine need in the market, can command a premium price. Price theory also tells us that whenever a product, by virtue of its uniqueness, can command supernormal profits, competitors often very quickly move in to reestablish a new market equilibrium at a more traditional profit level. See Figure 11-1 for summary of proposed pricing strategy for each type of new product.

## The Optimum Price

A thorough analysis of three dynamics, the product itself, the served market, and your competitors will increase the likelihood that you will choose the optimum price for your breakthrough product.

The optimum price has the following characteristics:

**Figure 11-1.** Alternative pricing strategies for new products.

---

| | |
|---|---|
| **Breakthrough:** | • Low keep-out pricing to maintain long-term advantage |
| | • "Skimming": High price/high profit on early sales |
| **"It's New for Us":** | • Gain market share via lowest price |
| | • Price competitively |
| | • Promote heavily |
| **New, Improved, Next Generation:** | • Up-charge from previous generation based on value |
| | • Price to the market target and specific prospects |
| **Line Extension:** | • Use accepted pricing formulas and monitor results |
| **3 *R*s:** | Repackaged |
| | • High price/heavy promotion |
| | • Competitive price, heavy public relations |
| | Repositioned |
| | • Heavy advertising |
| | • Advertising looks to reposition product line |
| | Recycled |
| | • Low volume, not high price |

---

1. It permits retailers or resellers to achieve their normal or expected margin.
2. It permits you to achieve your short- and long-term profit goal for the product.
3. The price is perceived by consumers as reasonable given the features and benefits of the product.
4. The price is sufficiently low or sufficiently competitive with currently available substitutes to persuade competitors against making the upfront time, money, and people-power investment necessary to market an "it's new for us" product competitor to your product.

Very few products in our experience score anywhere close to 100 percent on all four criteria of the optimum price. However, each proposed price for a major new product should be analyzed against each of these four criteria. Any pricing strategy that fails badly on one or more of the four criteria should be discarded.

The usual strategy for most breakthrough products or new, improved, next-generation products is to price them somewhat higher than established products. Several good arguments support following this strategy in many situations:

- The novelty and the newness can often command a premium with many buyers.
- The status seeker, the forerunner, or the first person on the block to try the newest toy is often the prime market for a breakthrough product in its early stages. This person is a label buyer who will gladly pay up for a new product, so why not get the upcharge?
- Production capacity is often limited, and the economics of experience curve pricing are not yet available, since the company is still moving up the learning curve on the new product.
- Rejects may be high. Recalls may be necessary and production costs may well be significantly higher than for established products. Therefore, a premium price is often not an option, but a necessity, if the new product is to cover its cost and make its initial profit projection.
- A high price often lends prestige to the product and helps to position it as a status product.
- Special product introduction costs can be sizeable and must be recovered one way or another, certainly in the long run but preferably in the short run.
- You can always crop the price if there is price resistance, but it is very hard to explain a price increase to customers.
- If a new product is priced too low relative to its perceived value in the marketplace one of two things happens:

    1. Retailers who resell the product add on an extra markup of their own above your retail list price. They

therefore get the "supernormal profit" that is the rightful fruit of your labor.

2. The product is sold out very quickly and goes into backorder.

- Assuming you have met your margin and profit needs, it is wise to price the new product at such a point where your sales force, your distributors, and your retailers still have to do some selling of the features and benefits of the new product.

The proper role of sales reps or distributors in the process of bringing new products to market is to convince retailers or end customers that this great new product is indeed worth any premium price asked for it in the marketplace.

There are also some arguments for bringing out some kinds of new products at a modest premium or no premium relative to available substitute products. Primarily this situation obtains when the product can be easily duplicated by competitors in a short time. Again, analysis of likely reactions of specific competitors is key in this situation.

"It's new for us" products must be priced based on the realities of the marketplace, rather than on your cost of bringing the product to market.

New, improved, next-generation products can sometimes command a modest upcharge from the price of the last generation model.

## The New Product and Product Line Pricing

Line extension products generally follow a preestablished pattern or relate to the value added or the cost saved relative to production of the line extension product. For example, large economy-sized packages are priced at a lower cost per ounce or pound than the standard size. Conversely, the pocket size or the "portion for one" size usually bears a higher per unit price since packaging is a larger percentage of total cost.

Step-up models or luxury models usually can be marketed

at a higher gross profit margin than the standard model. Step-down models or no frills/bare bones models often must carry a lower gross margin for all concerned to make them attractive to the bargain-conscious shopper.

Product line pricing is an exercise in balancing and trade-off analysis and good business judgment. The average gross profit of the sales of the entire line must reach certain targets, e.g., 35 percent, to achieve the profit plan. But the distribution of the price points of various models or overall gross margin of various items in the line may not reflect the actual variations in the cost of production or marketing. However, as long as estimates of sales by model are on target, the overall profit projection will usually be reasonably on target.

Fitting the new product or the line extension item smoothly into the pricing pattern is a fine art. In our experience, line sales and marketing managers who are close to the customer often do this better than do cost accountants and financial executives, who often are not in tune with the psychology of the marketplace and the likely reactions of competitors to the new product.

# CHAPTER TWELVE

# Advertising Strategies for New Products

For major new products including all breakthrough products, most "it's new for us" products, and some new, improved, next-generation and line extension products, an advertising budget, media plan, and positioning strategy should be established, at least on a tentative basis, early in the new product planning cycle.

There are several good reasons for doing this early in the process.

First, the act of setting an advertising budget also forces a focus on setting a sales budget for the new product in units and dollars for the first several years of sales.

Second, this exercise has the effect of getting the marketing people to make commitments regarding the role of advertising compared to other key elements in the marketing mix.

Third, the act of developing a product positioning and an advertising and promotion strategy for the new product requires marketing and product development people to prioritize the features and benefits of the product.

Fourth, this work also helps focus the efforts of the product development team, forcing them to concentrate their time and efforts on the products features and benefits that really make a difference, and preparing the positioning of the product against key competitors.

The choice of the proper advertising strategy and its timely execution in the right media is critical to the success of the new product introduction.

For consumer package goods products, the advertising positioning (the choice of the right message to communicate to the consumer) is often the single most important factor in the life or death struggle for supermarket shelf space and consumer acceptance.

For discretionary consumer products or big ticket items, for many industrial products, and for a wide range of services, the choice of the right advertising message and of the best media mix in which to present this message are also of critical importance.

Rather than attempt to present a primer on advertising for new products, I will briefly outline and contrast the critical issues that need to be addressed when you are deciding on your advertising strategy for products in each of our five categories of new products.

## Breakthrough Products

Most breakthrough products, from biotechnology and aerospace to the most mundane, require some level of market makeready, customer education, or, most important, behavior modification—a new set of expectations or relationships with the product or service. The compact disc, for example, required that consumers be informed of the need to purchase a new piece of audio equipment, along with use, care, and storage instructions for the discs as well as some behavior modifications on the part of the customers.

When an upscale, well-educated audience has one or more specific life-style characteristics (e.g., audiophiles, exercise and diet enthusiasts), the use of specialty print media is often recommended for breakthrough products. Print advertising can often be effective in explaining complex concepts or providing the information consumers require before making a major purchase decision.

Often, the breakthrough product has its own advertising budget and will be advertised separately and distinctly from other products in your line. It may also utilize a separate media mix and sometimes a specially dedicated creative and client services team at the advertising agency is required. For a breakthrough product that will depend heavily on advertising for its product launch, it is recommended that you bring your advertising agency people into the planning process at an early date. However, because advertising agency personnel turnover is high, only senior and responsible agency personnel should be permitted to attend confidential planning meetings. If the breakthrough product is aimed at a different target market or market segment than your normal customer mix, it is also advisable to involve media specialists from the agency at an early point in the process.

It is likely that the content, positioning, and media strategy for your breakthrough product will change as the product moves through the various stages of its life cycle. As the product becomes better known, moves into a mass or large market stage, and especially as it begins to attract competitors and imitators, your advertising strategy, approach, media plan, and expenditure level will all change, and they may need to change drastically and suddenly.

All large agencies and many small ones have senior people who have been involved with a range of breakthrough products through the various stages of the products' life cycle. While the products may be different, often these people can offer valuable street-smart advice that can save costly mistakes, but only if you bring them into the new product planning process at the proper time.

## "It's New for Us" Products

Commonly the "it's new for us" product relies more heavily on advertising expertise, or magic if you will, for its success than does any other category of new product.

When you are late coming to market, and your product offers nothing essentially different from what is already readily available, often the only real competitive weapons that you have are a lower price (read lower profit margin) or an advertising program that at least can create the illusion of a difference where none may exist in reality. The various brands of soap, detergent, cosmetics, shampoo, and—the most extreme example—243 brands of cigarettes spend billions of dollars each year to create illusory differences, euphemistically called product positionings, that motivate consumers to buy one brand over another. Seasoned packaged goods marketers can cite hundreds of examples when a change of advertising message has resulted in dramatic shifts in the brand's share of market for everything from cat food to flypaper.

If your new product is one that we must classify as "it's new for us," you must devote considerable energy, attention, and resources to an advertising plan that will help to distinguish your product from the already established competitors.

## New, Improved, Next-Generation Products

Media advertising is critical in explaining to consumers why the new, improved next-generation product is the one they should switch their purchases to. And for the large majority of new, improved, next-generation products, good advertising works.

Most customers, both left-brain industrial engineers who buy products on specifications and right-brain consumers who often buy products that fill emotional as well as material needs, are eagerly looking for the product that is newer, bigger, better in some way.

A skillful advertising message both kindles this passion for the new and shows in messages, direct and subliminal, how this new product does indeed provide something important that the old product did not.

## Line Extension Products

The line extension product typically has less reliance on advertising than do the other types of new products. Often the line extension product can be introduced at trade shows or sales meetings without major advertising expenditure. However, in retail situations, the successful introduction of the line extension product often requires that the retailer provide it with shelf space or display space. In such cases, it is vital that the shelf space allocated to the line extension product be *incremental* space and not space taken away from another product in your line. When the line extension product can only be introduced by cannibalizing shelf space from your established products, that is a good sign that it will cannibalize sales as well and may make only a very marginal contribution to total sales of the line. In such cases, the net profit contribution of the line extension product, if all expenses are properly allocated, is likely to be negative.

Trade advertising is usually effective for line extension products, which typically don't require high-intensity dedicated advertising programs.

## 3 *R*s

The *repackaged* product usually needs some modest amount of dedicated advertising. But it especially needs strong in-store display, if the new packaging is going to be noticed by customers.

*Repositioned* products by definition require a major marketing effort that usually involves a significant advertising program. Consumer goods products that are successfully repositioned can often score significant sales gains as new markets and new applications are opened up.

One of our advertising colleagues scored a major repositioning success with Snickers, the Mars candy bar that has been on the market for over fifty years. Through some investigative research, he determined that Snickers fit the official nutrition definition of a "snack food." He then developed a series of television commercials that depicted various workers both in offices and "he-man outdoor" situations taking a 4 PM energy break by eating Snickers. The advertising has now been running successfully for over three years.

*Recycled* products typically take on a different function than they had in their first product life cycle. Often they are modest recyclings that move the product upstream to cater to a very special niche market, usually smaller than the original market.

# CHAPTER THIRTEEN

# Naming the New Product

Sometimes a new product is so powerful or so unique that it can go to market with a very mundane name, often a compromise name concocted by a committee, and still be successful.

Mercedes-Benz is hugely successful in the marketing of luxury automobiles and they don't even bother to give names to their models, using instead numbers like 370, 450, and 580 that convey magical messages to motorists whose preference runs to "driving machines" rather than mere automobiles.

Toyota, in contrast, names its cars Celica, Camry, Corolla—names presumably generated by a computer or with letters left over from a Scrabble game, and they are, in their segment of the market, equally successful.

In the past few years, several new lines of cars have been introduced that employ evocative and symbolic names as part of their market positioning. Acura has achieved superior performance ratings that give credibility to its name. Infiniti uses surrealistic image advertising to distinguish itself from the general run of cars. Geo implies solid earthiness and Lexus has meaning to older, affluent professionals who once struggled with Latin.

Indeed, most industrial products come to market with names often prosaic, esoteric, or pedantic, but seldom elegant, imaginative, or clever, and it doesn't seem to "make no nevermind."

However, for most consumer products and for many industrial products and services, a catchy, memorable, or aptly descriptive name can make a big difference.

There is an esoteric but very professional branch of the marketing art known as nomenclature and symbology development. The people who practice this art, most of whom work for the major corporate identity consultants (e.g., Landor, Lippincott and Margulies, Lee and Young, Lefkowith, AGP), have developed a process and a methodology for generating names for new products and for companies. Names as diverse as Ameritech, Navistar, and Pampers have emerged from this process.

For every major new product introduction and for every launch that has serious dollars riding on the outcome, a specialist in nomenclature should be consulted by the product development team. This person can introduce a multistep discipline and methodology that will result in the choice of a name far superior to one chosen by the usual "hit and miss" methods used by so many companies.

The name selected should help to position the product and should be one that, for one reason or another, is memorable.

Some examples of new product names that, in my judgment, were a major factor in the successful introduction of the product or service include the following:

- *Cadillac Seville*—Elegant in its own right, but also traded smartly off the already established Sedan de Ville name.
- *Laserdisc*—Chosen by Pioneer for the optical videodisc player and accompanying software. Some may quibble about my listing this product with the Winners. More on this later.
- *Amtrak*—Chosen for the National Consumer Railway System to replace the original name, Rail Pax.
- *Nylon, Rayon, and more recently Corian*—Examples of very successful names that DuPont has generated using a proprietary process for naming new chemical formulations.

Other companies that have had special success in naming new products include Apple Computer and McDonalds. Apple has cleverly played off its name with MacSoft and Macintosh. McDonalds has taken a similar product family approach with its Chicken McNuggets and McBLT. More recent but less well known has been the development of McStops, a family-oriented motel and service station, which has an adjoining McDonalds franchise.

Perhaps the product category that currently best exemplifies the power of the name in creative marketing of the product is microcomputer software.

Microsoft seems logical enough, but LOTUS 1-2-3, which has no logical connection with computer software, has also been very successful. Microsoft has used WINDOWS, a simple but powerful image word, to designate its excellent graphics capability. More recently, software marketers have tapped into historical figures such as Socrates and Plato to provide imaginative word pictures and positionings for their software offerings, and one of the more sophisticated software program languages has been named after the French philosopher Pascal.

When the company envisions a breakthrough product as eventually developing into a line or a family of products, it is well advised to follow the lead of Apple, McDonalds, and Microsoft and develop names that can become the basis for a family of related names for the expanded product line.

# Mini-Histories

# 9

## The Cabbage Patch Kids

## From the Cabbage Patch Straight to Your Heart

In 1983, Coleco had a spectacular failure with the Adam Computer, and an equally spectacular success with the Cabbage Patch Kids doll. Introduced without fanfare, the Cabbage Patch Kids went on to become the single most successful product introduction in the history of the toy business.

The Cabbage Patch Kids concept was developed by Xavier Roberts, a "good ol' Georgia boy," who sold the dolls at very high prices as collectibles. Coleco negotiated a licensing arrangement with Roberts in 1983 and immediately subjected the Cabbage Patch Kids to intensive focus group research. Ruth Manko, an expert in the arcane art of conducting focus groups with children, was retained for this work. The research indicated the product had near-universal acceptance among parents, small girls, and even young boys.

The concept of the adoption of the Cabbage Patch Kid and the fact that the Kid came complete with two names was skillfully utilized in the market introduction to provide a unique positioning for the product. Preoccupied with its Adam home computer, Coleco management consistently underestimated the market demand of the Cabbage Patch Kid for the first two years. This proved a blessing in disguise as the Cabbage Patch Kid was the present most sought-after by small children for at least two consecutive Christmas seasons.

The official marketing effort was deliberately understated and word of mouth advertising and tons of free media publicity kept the Cabbage Patch Kid rolling for over four years. Total sales ran well over 30 million units and well over $1 billion at manufacturers' dollars.

Because they accomplished brilliant research, built a unique market positioning, and followed the game plan with a discipline rare to the toy business, Coleco was rewarded with a Big Winner in its Cabbage Patch Kid market introduction.

## Key Lesson

A company can be pursuing a brilliant strategy in one product category even as it is sowing the seeds of disaster in a second product category. Brilliance and folly can coexist in the same company at the same time. Cabbage Patch Kids was not a lucky break, as some have insisted. Coleco had a brilliant plan for the doll, and it was executed brilliantly.

## Postscript

The fact that some companies such as Coleco and Cuisinart that managed brilliant product introductions later went into Chapter 11 bankruptcy in no way diminishes the glory of their accomplishment or the value of the lessons they provide us.

# 10

## The Block Automation System

### When the Culture Doesn't Support New Product Introduction

The New York Stock Exchange (NYSE) is an American institution that dates back to 1792. As the operator of the largest stock exchange in the world, the NYSE serves as the rulemaker and stabilizer of the securities industry.

Such an institution comes to the act of bringing new products to market only with great difficulty. During the late 1960s the Exchange decided to design and introduce an electronic system to facilitate the trading of large blocks of stock. This system required member firms to input their large block trades into the system which advertised the availability of these blocks, while preserving the identity of the offering firm.

When I joined the Exchange as business planning manager, the Block Automation System had been in operation for several years and had lost some millions of dollars during this startup period.

My assignment was to analyze the long-term potential of the system and to recommend a plan for bringing the system to profitability or to recommend an orderly phase-out, if a turnaround could not be achieved in a reasonable time.

The state of the art of the electronic technology as of 1972 was not sufficiently advanced to permit the kind of near-instantaneous callup of data that is required by hard-driving fund managers and block traders. Plagued by operational problems, the Block Automation System was considered to be too slow, too incomplete in its listing of major stock positions, and too expensive to meet the needs of a very demanding customer base. Ironically, many member firms were of the opinion that this service should be provided free as a perquisite of their NYSE membership.

Perhaps most important, the managers involved, who

operated in a culture that emphasized high standards of service, integrity, and stability, were ill cast in the role of entrepreneurs charged with bringing new products to market. The normal rewards of entrepreneurship were not available to them, nor was the freedom to make quick decisions necessary to a new product introduction permitted in the Stock Exchange of the early 1970s.

So a breakthrough product, developed at great cost, was allowed to expire because the timing was wrong and the culture of the Exchange was wrong for bringing new products to market. At another time, under a new chairman, Mil Batten, the NYSE learned to create and develop successful new services. By that time, I had left for a more entrepreneurial world and the Block Automation System had been laid to rest.

Thus, despite great expenditures of time and effort by many dedicated people, the Block Automation System, a breakthrough product, must be classified with the Losers.

## Key Lesson

The proper culture for introducing new products must be in place before you can be successful in marketing new products. Companies ruled by entrenched bureaucracies are not destined for success in an entrepreneurial type of business. You need to accurately analyze the prevailing business culture before you can compete on Wall Street in financial services.

# 11

## Michelin Tire

# We Couldn't Afford Anything Less

As a young midtown Manhattan resident who used cabs and rental cars as a primary means of locomotion, I considered automobile tires to be the penultimate commodity product. They were all made in Akron, Ohio, and Goodyear and Goodrich sounded like interchangeable parts. Thus, on moving to suburban New Jersey and acquiring my first real car, I was surprised when my wife, a sophisticated marketing professional, insisted that the new car have only Michelin tires, regardless of the cost.

Valuing family harmony more than the upcharge involved, I agreed and have been happily riding on Michelins ever since.

A recent chance meeting with a former marketing executive of Michelin allowed me to probe the mystery of why Michelin tires have been so successful in carving out a high-end niche in what I had once supposed was a commodity market.

Michelin did indeed have a superior product when they entered the U.S. market. The steel-belted radial tire based on technology that had been available to Americans was first perfected and brought to market by this French firm. But the American manufacturers were busy marketing lower-priced bias ply tires to the mass market. They did not think that steel-belted radials selling at a substantial upcharge from the standard tire constituted a significant market. Michelin had several years to establish its preemptive positioning as the Rolls-Royce (or perhaps the Volvo) of the tire industry before the Americans realized they had to compete for this steel-belted radial business.

Michelin no longer has the clear-cut product superiority that it had during those early years, but the company wisely invested in image advertising along the way. The concept that

Michelin means safety for your family, and this safety is worth an upcharge, appears now to be firmly embedded in the consciousness of many American consumers.

So by recognizing that new technology can create upscale niches even in commodity markets, and by consistently communicating its message to the target market, Michelin has created a Big Winner for itself in the U.S.

## Key Lesson

A superior technology can be successful in an established commodity market and still command an upcharge in price, so long as there is a compelling reason for the upcharge (such as the safety of your family) which is communicated clearly and distinctly in your advertising program. But most important, the large, bureaucratic American competitors failed to react quickly to Michelin's new product initiative, giving it time to solidify its position in the high end of the market.

# 12

## Automated Teller Machines

### When a New Technology Creates Both New Markets and New Marketing Problems

Automated teller machines (ATMs) were introduced by banks in the early 1970s, when technology made it possible to automatically debit and credit customers' accounts from remote locations. ATMs are yet another example of a major new breakthrough product that has required substantial education of the customer, and a substantial behavior modification on the part of many customers before ATMs became an accepted part of their life-style.

ATMs were originally embraced by banks for cash saving reasons. For a one-time investment of approximately $75,000 per unit, the bank was in effect hiring a lifetime, twenty-four-hour-a-day, seven-day-a-week bank teller.

The ATM concept was also perceived to provide several additional benefits to consumer banks. First, it was the expectation of bank management and a major selling point of the ATM marketers that the machines would be used largely to service the low-volume transactions of poor, elderly, inner-city customers whose business was becoming increasingly costly to service via live tellers. Second, the ATM was expected to have widespread appeal to the young, affluent, time-conscious, and convenience-oriented upper-income customer. Those people would presumably welcome the convenience factor of banking at odd hours and on weekends.

The experience of ten-plus years with ATM machines has proved that the ATM has largely been rejected by older, low-income customers, who are put off by new technology and, most important, highly prize the socialization with tellers that bank management had hoped to restrict.

The second target market group has overwhelmingly accepted ATM use, beyond the original expectations of the bankers. And therein lies a problem for the banks. These high-income, fast-moving young people are prime targets for a wide range of banking services such as certificates of deposit, mortgages, car loans, second mortgages, or credit lines.

Typically, these services require some degree of personalized selling. To a considerable extent sales of these banking services are facilitated by reminders from tellers, the ready availability of platform officers, and the smorgasbord of brochures, statement stuffers, signs, and displays that adorn the local bank branch. But when your prime prospect for these services becomes conditioned to do his or her basic banking in the still of the night, interacting only with a machine that has a very limited program menu, much of this other business can be lost.

There are now well over 85,000 ATMs in service in America and they are indeed a permanent part of the banking landscape. But to the product managers and market managers for the specialized high-profit products noted above, ATMs are a problem that has made them compete aggressively for business that, in a simpler past, would have been generated "over the transom" in that cozy neighborhood branch.

## Key Lesson

A major new technology that requires life-style changes will not necessarily be accepted equally well by all segments of your market. And when the new technology tends to reduce cross-sell synergy for other products and services, you may have to increase your marketing costs just to maintain your business.

On balance, we must classify the ATM with the Big Winners. The convenience such machines provide is valued by customers and the dramatic reduction in bank teller labor costs is a godsend to the profit-stressed banks. But the need to expend additional marketing costs (e.g., direct mail and advertising) to recapture the lost "over the transom" business indicates that ATMs are not an unmixed blessing. The ATM fulfilled some but not all of the strategic objectives that had been established for it.

# 13

## The Psychedelic Sunscreen

## The Importance of the Product Manager

Zinc oxide, the stark white ointment that acts as a total sun-screen, has long been the trademark of the lifeguard. Several years ago, an imaginative Australian entrepreneur decided to market a line of zinc oxide sun screens in a riot of different colors.

Our client, himself a very imaginative entrepreneur, saw these psychedelic sunscreens on a number of young people at Bondi Beach in Australia and immediately acquired the rights to market the product in the United States.

Our assignment was to analyze the potential U.S. market, to develop a market entry plan and a strategy, and to assist the product manager hired by our client to manage the introduction. Our analysis of the sunscreen market indicated that zinc oxide accounted for a very small and declining share of a market that was dominated by several large, aggressive firms. Most important, the traditional way of doing business in this market was for retailers to take product early in the year on consignment, receive extended dating terms, and have the right to return unsold product at the end of the summer season. Not exactly a scenario made to order for a startup company.

We recommended the product be positioned as a multi-purpose "fun" product for young people. It could be used as a sunscreen for summer bathing or on the ski slopes, and as "punk party paint" at any time of the year. Distribution was planned through upscale cosmetics departments in leading department stores that would permit a large margin for promotion.

Several immediate problems arose however, to frustrate this plan. First, the timing of the startup was too tight to allow for manufacture and distribution of the first shipments in time for the upcoming summer season. Second, and more critical, a product manager had been hired who had no previous experience in the product category or in the many disciplines of product management. While diligent and hard-working, the product manager was overwhelmed by the many duties involved in bringing a new product to market in a very seasonal, time-critical situation.

For example, a package design needed to be created, a contract packager identified and retained, an advertising program and media schedule developed, and a point of sale demonstration program initiated, all within a tight time span.

Despite an imaginative marketing promotion program, it was a case of too little, too late for the psychedelic sunscreen. At this point, we must classify the psychedelic sunscreen as a Loser. The acceptance level as a novelty was excellent and a reintroduction with more time for planning could still establish this product as a Modest Winner.

## Key Lesson

Product management is a high-skill profession. Success in this demanding profession requires that the practitioner possess both the necessary technical or academic skills as well as real-life experience on the new product firing line. This is not a position for which on-the-job training alone is sufficient for success.

# 14

## The Original Xerox Copier

### Starting the Revolution in Office Automation

In the early 1950s a small Rochester, New York, firm called the Haloid Company acquired rights to the xerographic process of copying. Battelle Institute was commissioned to conduct product development work and Stewart Dougall and Associates, a marketing consulting firm, was retained to conduct market research and to help plan the market introduction.

The story, as related to me years later by colleagues at Stewart Dougall, goes as follows:

- The market research was extensive and indicated that the demand for the first Xerox copiers, which were primitive compared to the models available today, was far beyond the expectations of the Haloid Company or their capacity to produce. However, the costs of the first models would be high, in excess of $4,000.
- Xerox management, recognizing that it had a product for which the demand was truly unlimited, but only if the product could be made affordable, conceived a brilliant but very simple strategy for establishing the Xerox copier. Copiers would be placed with customers and paid for on a usage or copy basis rather than through a high upfront purchase price.

The combination of a revolutionary breakthrough product, a unique pricing concept, and a first-rate marketing and service organization has fueled the growth of the $13 million dollar Haloid Company of the early 1950s into the $10 billion-plus Xerox Corporation of the late 1980s.

The xerographic process developed into a unique product that helped create the office of today and was the forerunner of the age of office automation.

A Big Winner in every respect.

## Key Lesson

A product can be a revolutionary breakthrough that provides quantum leap advantages over currently available products but it still must be affordable. When the Xerox copier was first introduced, the sophisticated equipment leasing industry of today did not exist. Xerox needed an ingenious approach to making their copier affordable and found it through the "pay for use" concept. The use of imaginative pricing as a marketing strategy helped propel Xerox to a great success.

# 15

## Advent Projection Television
### The Lonely Road of the True Innovator

Henry Kloss is recognized as one of the true geniuses of the consumer electronics industry. Founder of four entrepreneurial companies in an industry dominated by giants, Henry Kloss was responsible for a number of technical breakthroughs in the stereo hi-fi industry in its early days. Turning his creative and technical talents to video, Henry formed Advent Corporation with the goal of designing, producing, and marketing projection TV systems.

Truly a breakthrough product, the first projection television systems utilized advanced lens technology and unique product design to provide 60- and 72-inch projection systems. The high costs and the bulkiness of the first systems restricted their market acceptance primarily to public places such as bars, private clubs, and a small number of well-to-do individuals.

When I analyzed this business in the late 1970s, annual unit sales of projection television systems were still under 100,000 units and prices were in the $5,000-and-up range.

Advent retained a dominant share of this small but growing market through the late 1970s. The company was plagued, however, by high costs and lack of capital to build the production capability necessary to drastically reduce costs or to generate sufficient advertising to stimulate consumer demand.

The resignation of Henry Kloss, the acquisition of the company by Peter Sprague, and the installation of Bernie Mitchell, a dynamic marketing executive who had propelled Pioneer from an unknown firm to the leadership position in the hi-fi industry, were widely regarded as signaling the turnaround of Advent.

However, the manufacturing, inventory control, and general operational problems of the company were of such dimensions that this talented turnaround team was unable to turn the company around before the banks moved in. It later became known that because of the lack of cost controls and poor pricing policies, Advent was losing money on each unit shipped at a time when they dominated the market.

A Chapter 11 reorganization was unavailing and ultimately the company was forced out of the projection TV business, just as the product category was reaching the critical mass in terms of sales volume and market acceptance that might have permitted survival.

Thus, a major breakthrough product pioneered by a small entrepreurial company was ultimately a Loser. Its downfall was due neither to competition nor to poor quality but to the failure to build the necessary strength in the areas of finance, inventory control, and systems that would match the brilliance of the company's technology and creativity. And the turnaround team came in too late to rescue the company.

## Key Lesson

A small company with limited resources must watch its costs and finances very closely, even when it has a market niche all to itself. Avant-garde products such as the Advent Novabeam projection TV of the late 1970s can command a premium price in the marketplace. Recognizing that their window of opportunity was narrow, Advent should have concentrated on earning a profit rather than building a market for others. Failure to "price for value" led to financial disaster.

# 16

## Learning Disabilities Treatment Centers

When Partners With Incompatible Goals Fail to Produce the Necessary Startup Capital

It is now estimated that one in seven American school children suffers from some mild or severe learning disability. Dyslexia, the most commonly used term to describe learning disabilities, is actually an umbrella term for the literally hundreds of variations of learning disabilities that have been catalogued or diagnosed to date. All but the most wealthy and most sophisticated school systems lack the specialized people, equipment, and expertise needed to treat even the most elementary and commonplace of these many forms of learning disabilities.

A number of entrepreneurial companies which were subsequently acquired by larger firms have attempted to provide treatment or remediation for the lesser forms of dyslexia or learning disability. Sylvan Learning Centers, acquired by Kinder Care, and Huntington Learning Centers were the established leaders in providing remedial and tutorial services to students with learning difficulties.

Several years ago, I was introduced to two people who recognized the growing need in this area and who were planning to build a national chain of centers where trained practitioners would work one-on-one or in small groups with learning-disabled students.

At first glance the two partners seemed to be a good pairing. Friends since college days, one was a learning disabilities professional with management experience. His colleague was a highly entrepreneurial individual who had extensive experience in tax shelters, real estate, and financial markets.

The assignment, which was to analyze the market opportunity and prepare the business plan, came unraveled due to the incompatible goals and styles of the partners. The learning disabilities professional wanted a small, top-of-the-line professional organization that he could personally manage and control. The entrepreneur wanted to ramp up quickly to the status of a national chain and to sell franchises to achieve this goal.

I recommended establishing two pilot learning centers in a major West Coast market. This plan came unglued when the founders were unwilling to personally finance the test market and unable to gain the necessary startup financing from other sources.

Thus a startup company which had a concept with the potential to be at least a Modest Winner produced instead a Loser, even though the entrepreneurs had hit on a need for which the market has been proved to exist and which is growing rapidly.

## Key Lesson

Establishing a new business as a "partnership" in which two entrepreneurs have equal voice is a path fraught with danger. The three critical variables, *all of which* must be positive for a partnership to succeed, are:

1. Complementary skills
2. Compatible styles
3. Congruent goals

In the case of the Learning Disabilities Treatment Centers, the first two criteria were satisfied but the last criterion of congruent goals certainly was not. This is a case where the "people side" of a new product introduction was the undoing.

# 17

## Consumer Optical Videodisc

### The Long Lonely March to Establish a Major New Technology

The RCA capacitance videodisc player was a poor idea that failed despite brilliant execution (see Mini-History 3). The consumer optical videodisc system, introduced with great fanfare in late 1979, still struggles to establish itself as a major new breakthrough product. It is widely accepted that optical videodisc (also called Laserdisc) provides a picture and sound quality inherently superior to that provided by the vastly more popular videocassette recorder (VCR).

Further, optical videodiscs provide the capability of offering slow motion, stop action, frame by frame access and the ability to almost instantly access any portion of the disc. Perhaps most important, the videodisc picture quality does not degrade with repeated playing, as does the videocassette.

In spite of all these advantages, the VCR outsells the optical videodisc player by an order of magnitude of about one hundred to one. There are many reasons for this imbalance, but the one most commonly advanced does not hold up when subjected to research and analysis.

"The problem with the videodisc is it doesn't record" is almost always advanced as the reason why Americans choose the VCR over the optical videodisc player. Research by our company and others confirms that over half of the VCR owners do not use the record feature at all and use their VCRs solely or almost entirely to play prerecorded movie cassettes that they rent or, increasingly, purchase from video stores or other retailers. Faced with these realities, Pioneer, the dominant supplier of Laserdisc hardware and software, has properly positioned the Laserdisc player as a prestige item sold to affluent, upscale consumers who already own a videocassette recorder.

While much of the world thinks of the consumer videodisc player as a Loser  Pioneer quietly perseveres as only a Japanese company can, secure in the knowledge that superior technology and perseverance will eventually reward it with a Big Winner.

## Key Lesson

Breakthrough products often require an extended market makeready period before they are accepted by customers. No product in my experience has had a longer market makeready than the optical videodisc player. As of early 1990, the optical videodisc is finally beginning to receive strong popular acceptance in the American marketplace. Sales are up over 100 percent, and other major Japanese consumer electronics firms are now starting to promote the videodisc player, since its time finally seems to have arrived.

# 18

## *Automotive Week*

## Establishing the "Green Sheet" as the Voice of the Auto Aftermarket

In the Information Age of the 1980s, the newsletter developed into the fastest growing and most cost-effective means of reaching specialized audiences with unique information needs. More than 10,000 newsletters are now published in the United States. Few have started more simply or been more effective in serving their market than *Automotive Week.*

Founded in 1975, *Automotive Week* was literally a kitchen-table operation until its success required moving to larger quarters. The newsletter has positioned itself as the voice of the auto aftermarket, providing early alerts on significant new trends, mergers and re-organizations, personnel changes, and other items of interest to auto aftermarket retailers, manufacturers, sales representatives, and industry analysts.

The founder and editor/publisher had the ideal background to bring this new product to market. Trained as a financial desk reporter with the *New York Journal-American* of happy memory, he then spent some years as writer and editor for various automotive trade journals.

His strategic plan for establishing *Automotive Week* was simple but effective. He devoted several months to building a database of potential subscribers before publishing the first issue. He also provided free sample copies of the first newsletters to individuals attending various industry trade shows by personally slipping copies under hundreds of hotel room doors in Chicago and Las Vegas.

Use of a distinctive green paper has earned *Automotive Week* the name "Green Sheet" by which it is universally recognized in the auto aftermarket. A consistently high level of information and analysis, timed to hit the reader's desk on

Monday morning, has given *Automotive Week* a unique niche that larger publishers envy but are too wise to challenge. So because the founder took the slow but sure road to building a long-term business *Automotive Week* has become a Big Winner by providing a unique service to the $90 billion auto aftermarket.

## Key Lesson

To establish any new publishing venture is usually a long, slow process. The editor of *Automotive Week* recognized that he had to follow the same planning disciplines and market development approach that are used by large magazines. This includes market research, free sample issues, and timely introduction in the proper environment, in this case the major auto aftermarket industry trade shows.

## Winning Ideas

1. The role and expected profit contribution of new products should be explicitly spelled out in your company's strategy plan.
2. Companies that win at the new product game usually have a positive corporate culture in which bureaucracy and politics are subordinate to common goals.
3. The selection of the best person to manage a new product is critical to its success and must not be made lightly.
4. Early sales results should be monitored closely and compared to the new products proforma P&L to validate success or identify early problems with market acceptance.
5. Most new products, especially breakthrough products, should be priced at a premium and often a substantial premium above currently existing products.
6. It is useful to have a working version of an advertising plan early in the process to help the product development team focus on delivering features and benefits of importance to customers.
7. When serious money is at stake it is wise to employ experienced professionals to select the name for your new product.

# SECTION III

# MARKET RESEARCH FOR NEW PRODUCTS

Studies of the reasons new products fail in the marketplace always list the absence of market research as a prime cause of failure.

I would add the failure to perform the right kind of research, to ask the right questions of the right people, and to draw the proper conclusions from the research data, in addition to sloppy, unprofessional interviewing—all are important reasons for the failure of new products.

This section will discuss, in some detail, the various types of research that are likely to be most effective, the situations where each should be utilized, and the strengths and limitations of each type of research.

# CHAPTER FOURTEEN
# It All Starts With the Customer

We all know that the end customer has the power of life and death over new products. All the wizardry of Madison Avenue cannot save a new product that does not deliver what it promises, that is perceived as highly overpriced. or that fails to address any need, real or perceived, of the customer.

Yet I am constantly amazed that companies, large and small, invest huge sums of money in new product planning, developing prototypes, creating package designs, preparing advertising programs, and generating profit and sales projections, often with little or no input from the retailer, distributor, or end customer.

Various reasons are advanced for why companies so often neglect or slight the act of receiving feedback from customers as part of the new product planning process:

• *Plain old-fashioned arrogance.* Many entrepreneurs especially think they know their customers' needs better than do the customers themselves, so why bother to ask?

A corollary to this is the idea that "we are such great marketers or salesmen, that surely we will be able to meet the sales quota on this new product."

• *No time, no money for talking to customers.* Time constraints

are often advanced as reasons for finessing the step of customer research. In fact, even a complex national probability survey can usually be completed in a fraction of the time it takes
to bring the new product to market readiness.

The money issue is also an argument that falls of its own
weight. In my experience it is rare that even a definitive
market research and analytical study adds more than 1 or 2
percent to the total cost of the new product introduction.

• *Can't trust customers to give accurate feedback.* This mindset
is often found in companies that have been burned by poor-
quality, sloppy market research and analysis in the past. Surveys that asked the wrong questions, or studies that talked to
the wrong people rather than the true decision maker; inter-
viewers who failed to probe for the real reasons; analysts who
failed to properly weigh or assess research material; all these
and more could easily lead a company to misread the reaction
of the customer to a proposed new product.

But customers have no reason not to provide full and
accurate feedback on your new product ideas. If the new
product provides a value, feature, or benefit not currently
available, it is manifestly in their interest to provide positive
feedback to your product planning process. If the new product serves no purpose or is very overpriced it also serves the
customers' interest to give you this information.

• *Lack of knowledge of the appropriate research techniques to use.*
The first three objections noted above are deeply ingrained in
the culture of the company. They can be overcome only by
changing the attitude and values of top management relative
to research and new products.

This last objection is the only legitimate reason for not
conducting thorough market research and analysis early in the
new product planning process.

The balance of this section provides an overview of the
various research approaches appropriate for different new
product introductions.

# CHAPTER FIFTEEN

# Life-Style and Demographic Research

Herman Kahn, the late futurologist, prophesied in the early 1970s that the United States of the year 2000 would be a "mosaic society" composed of many distinct cultural and language groups. This prediction has already become a reality that market planners and product planners must constantly factor into their analyses.

The concept of the mass market has, in many situations, been superseded by a proliferation of niche markets.

Typically some combinations of an individual's life-style, which is the sum total of many factors and preferences, and his or her demographics (age, income, race, occupation, education level) goes a long way to determine the person's likely acceptance or rejection of any given new product. Even for industrial products, where reason and logic are supposedly dominant, purchase decisions are strongly colored by the preferences, life-styles, and values of the *individuals* who make these purchase decisions on behalf of their companies.

Life-style at first glance is an amorphous, all-embracing concept. But market analysts, demographers, and researchers have identified some key indicators that are useful for purposes of market analysis.

• *Where you are in the life cycle.* Such categories as young marrieds with no children, families with small children, empty nesters, and early retirees are useful categories for purposes of market analysis and new product planning.

The emergence of the "mature market" and the large growth in the number of people aged 60 and over have brought new challenges and new product opportunities to many companies.

• *Type and place of residence.* The growing trend toward owning condominiums and co-ops, the aging of suburbia, the movement to the Sunbelt, and the proliferation of retirement villages and summer home communities all are trends with important marketing implications.

• *Changing roles in male-female relationships.* Later marriages, deferred child bearing, smaller families, two-income families, yuppies, and dinks (double income, no kids) together with the trend toward working at home are among the many phenomena that need to be analyzed and understood relative to many new products.

• *Time/money tradeoffs and convenience products.* For many middle-class, middle-income, middle Americans, time is a commodity that is more scarce than money. Products and services that provide convenience, that save time, trouble, or hassle are often welcome on the market. It is important to refocus on the fact that many of today's most important new products are really services. The vast range of electronics and telecommunications products that have reached the market in the past decade are not "consumed" but rather enjoyed or used. They improve the quality of life and expand the range of options for work and leisure.

• *The emphasis on health, safety, nutrition, and health care.* A major life-style element that must be considered by marketers is the current emphasis on eating healthy, keeping fit, weight reduction, exercise, and alternate forms of nutrition and medicine. Allied to this is the ever-growing concern with ecology, air pollution, disposal of waste products, and other forms of conservation and "saving the planet." Any new product that rides on the waves of these life-style and values will have a greater likelihood of success. New products that run counter to those trends (e.g., beers, cigarettes, rich and high-calorie foods, liquors, firearms) will have a more uphill battle to achieve success in the marketplace of the 1990s.

# CHAPTER SIXTEEN

# Market Segmentation Analysis

Segmentation works at many different levels and it is the challenge of marketers to determine how much effort is practical to expend in order to determine which prospects should be targeted for purchase and in what order of priority.

The result can be as simple as identifying the sequential list of buyers or as complex as profiling the several groups of customer types that could purchase the new item.

In virtually every instance, it is wise to segment the potential customers for a new product into two or more groups that are "different" in ways that are measurable and that are important for you. A market segmentation analysis can be performed at many different levels of sophistication depending on the nature of the product, and the buying habits, needs, and preferences of the target market.

For industrial products or producers' goods for which there are relatively few customers, the segmentation can be performed by knowledgeable marketing managers without extensive research input. Often the segmentation for such products deals with the sequence and the timing with which your key customers will buy the new product. Potential customers for products such as machine tools, steel mill equipment, and jet aircraft can be segmented in this fashion.

For new consumer products in categories such as packaged foods, toiletries, and financial services, the market segmentation can become much more complex and sophisticated. Here, the proper starting point is usually the wealth of demographic data, initially developed in the decennial census and made available for a fee, to firms that specialize in demographics, life-style, and psychographic research.

Great progress has been made in the past decade in developing a number of basic consumer market segments, that have widespread application to many categories of new products. This process has been greatly assisted by the revolution in microcomputer technology and in new, fast methods of data storage and retrieval.

For example it is now possible, using various demographics services, to receive detailed information about such factors as age, income, life-style, and home ownership of consumers even at the level of the census block. It is possible to examine the mosaic referred to earlier right down to the zip code plus four-digit postal code level of detail. One segment, for example, might include only several floors of a large urban apartment building, a block on a suburban street, or a condominium development in the Sunbelt.

The households resident in each "cell" are classified based on similarities in consumer behavior, values, consumption, product use, and expenditure patterns.

Computer-based systems are widely available for integrating your own customer information and your own research studies with these external market data.

Today's advanced information technology is most highly refined among consumer markets, yet the principles applied to gain insight about that market are not dissimilar to those used when segmenting the industrial and commercial markets.

The major objectives of performing market segmentation are as follows:

1. Determine the potential or likelihood of a group of prospects for using and buying particular types of products and services, at various points in the product life-cycle.

2. Identify the segments that have the highest immediate potential for the new product.
3. Design targeted marketing communications programs to capture those prospects.

As noted, markets can be segmented in innumerable ways, but for the segmentation to be useful and actionable, the data must be translated into specific action steps or specific advertising programs. One brief example of an actionable segmentation follows:

NBO Stores, Inc., a leading retail men's clothing chain, had built its business as an off-price retailer. Faced with increased discounting by its department store competitors, NBO recognized the need to segment and analyze its customer base and to refine its merchandise mix.

A series of focus groups enabled NBO to develop a segmentation of the market based on life-style factors, the importance of clothing to various groups of men, and their reaction to the act of shopping for clothing. Different approaches to the merchandising and advertising and to the lines of clothing carried were developed, based on the reactions of different groups of consumers that were revealed in the focus groups.

# CHAPTER SEVENTEEN

# Focus Group Research

Focus group research is primarily designed to test the validity of a product concept before investing substantial time, money, and research effort into developing the product. Focus groups usually involve bringing together from eight to twelve participants, all of whom have been prescreened and all of whom meet certain objective criteria determined in advance.

The purpose of the focus group is to learn the in-depth, visceral reactions of respondents who represent the prime potential market to the features, benefits, styling, packaging, and pricing of the proposed new product.

For consumer focus groups it is important to select people who have not participated in a focus group before or at least not in the past several years. Participating in focus groups is fun and besides you are paid a participation fee. Therefore, some homemakers and retired people look on this activity as recreation and as a source of extra income. Unfortunately, "professional focus group participants" start to think and act like marketing advisors rather than as consumers and the value of their input is questionable.

Typically, focus group sessions are audiotaped and frequently videotaped, so that the company personnel and research consultants can review the findings in depth at a later date. It is a common practice for client company personnel to sit in an adjoining room with a one-way mirror so that they can see and hear the discussions "live" without the knowledge of the focus group participants.

The focus group is normally from 90 to 120 minutes in length, conducted by a professionally trained moderator, whose expertise is in psychology and group dynamics rather than in product development or marketing.

Focus group moderators are very well paid since this is an art that requires great people skill to practice successfully.

One or two overly aggressive, argumentative, or ill-informed focus group participants can often create an atmosphere where the purpose of the focus group is lost in confusion. The moderator must walk a fine line between being too controlling, in which case the desired free form discussion is inhibited, and being too permissive, in which case the discussion can wander far from the objectives of the focus group. The focus group moderator must be highly skilled in fostering the kind of creative interaction and often creative conflict between the focus group participants that allows us to get to the "bottom line" of what people like and don't like about the new product concept, along with the reasons for their reactions.

A product concept statement that clearly describes and explains the new product should be prepared, which is presented to the focus group participants during the session. It is often useful to provide product designs, mockups, and several proposed price points as inputs to the focus group respondents.

Focus group research is recommended for all proposed breakthrough products and for all new product concepts whose development would involve a substantial amount of time, money, and R&D effort. Industrial and high-tech products are also included in this category. Focus groups are usually not required for product line extensions or for products already well established in the market that a client is producing for the first time (the "it's new for us" product), but there are exceptions to all these statements.

Focus groups are highly regarded by many large advertising agencies as being useful in the positioning of new products against specific target markets.

Focus groups also serve as an insurance policy against bad ideas and can save significant amounts of money that would otherwise be invested in a bad new product idea. In one case that we were personally involved in, a large chain of retail stores was persuaded not to undertake a major redesign of its stores estimated to cost $20 million, based on a uniformly unfavorable reaction to the new concept in a series of focus groups.

Focus group research is meant to be directional, not definitive. However, in a large majority of cases, a professionally planned and conducted focus group will lay bare the fallacies of a bad product idea, so that management can either revise the concept to make it workable or put it to rest, saving much time and money.

A majority of the 85 percent of new product concepts that fail to make it to the market, and on which companies waste many billions of dollars per year, could be written off much earlier in the process if management had the wisdom to invest a moderate sum of money in professionally conducted focus group research.

The focus group approach is more recently being extended to industrial products, high-tech products, and business services where the group participants are business executives and professionals. It is not easy to get ten busy executives to commit to meet at a given time and place, and substantial incentive payments must be offered, but the results often justify the time and expense involved.

# CHAPTER EIGHTEEN
# Delphi Panels

In ancient Greece, the oracle at Delphi was consulted by rulers before they made a major decision. During the 1950s, the Rand Corporation, a major "think tank" primarily concerned with national security questions, devised the Delphi Research Technique. This technique has, since the early 1980s, been applied with success to an increasing number of new product introductions.

The Delphi Research Technique involves selecting a panel of the best and brightest and most qualified experts in a given field, to provide analysis and insight into the merits and the market potential of a new product. Delphi panels are especially valuable for technical breakthrough products, for which the target consumer often lacks the necessary experience or frame of reference to make an informed judgment. For example, a comprehensive Delphi project was conducted by a major university on the laser optical videodisc when this product was first being introduced to the market.

The choice of Delphi panel participants is critical. Typically, the panelists will be drawn on a judgment basis from among the following kinds of people:

- Sales managers, sales representatives, or stocking distributors
- Knowledgeable senior people at your best customers,

who can be relied upon to maintain confidence about your plans
- Scientists, professors, and industry experts who have the technical capability to evaluate the proposed product under consideration
- Knowledgeable trade media people and consultants who are technically qualified and who will keep this work in confidence
- Government researchers or analysts who may have studied the product category or market in question

The procedure to be followed in Delphi research includes the following:

1. A detailed description of the product and the concept is provided to each Delphi panel participant in the mail.

It should be noted that a comprehensive, multistep Delphi research program can be carried out by mail and telephone without bringing all the experts together as a group in one location. A list of questions or issues for discussion is also provided. Each participant is asked to return his/her data and completed questionnaire by a specified date.

2. All research data are then tabulated, analyzed, and summarized either manually or increasingly on a personal computer by the project manager.
3. A summary of this data analysis is then provided to each Delphi group participant.
4. Participants are then asked to review and, if appropriate, to modify their original answers based on their review of the consensus findings of the Delphi panel.

In other words, each expert is asked to give a second opinion, which may be the same or different from his first opinion, based on his or her analysis of the consensus findings of the expert panel.

5. The final revised data are then presented to management and to the product development people as being the consensus judgment of the expert panel.

Delphi research is especially valuable when the product concept is more or less unique and where it is necessary to have intensive expert or peer group review of its feasibility and marketability prior to committing to a major product development or R&D program.

Some business researchers dismiss Delphi research as too theoretical or time-consuming. Others are concerned about the confidentiality factor and the potential for premature disclosure of plans to people over whom one has no direct control. These are legitimate issues and indeed a Delphi study needs to be planned and designed with great care if it is to achieve its purpose. But this is a proven, relatively low-cost approach to receiving organized expert opinion on the prospects for a major new product.

# CHAPTER NINETEEN

# Test Markets

The practice of introducing new products in a test market mode has been commonplace in consumer package goods for many years. More recently the test market approach has been expanded to a number of consumer durables products, and to an increasing number of industrial products.

### When and Why Test Markets

1. *For breakthrough products that require some behavior modification or learning process by customers, the possibility of rejection of the new product or the new technology is always present.* A test market allows you to get feedback in a real-time mode, on how the cash customers react to the product in the actual selling environment. Sometimes minor modifications in the product design or in the descriptive literature can spell the difference between acceptance or rejection. Test markets can sniff out such problems and enable you to correct them prior to the full-scale launch.

2. *Operating in a test market mode is sometimes necessary for small or start-up companies that lack the resources to go into national distribution.* Often your bankers or venture financiers will want some hard evidence of market acceptance before they commit to the full level of funding needed to go national with the new product.

3. *The test market is still the best "disaster insurance" against a costly or potentially ruinous new product failure.* Probably the riskiest business known is the bringing of a new play to Broadway. For many years now, it has been standard practice to open new plays on the road, typically in New Haven or Philadelphia. If the show bombs totally, it is quietly closed and the loss to financial backers is minimized. If the reaction on the road indicates that reworking or further work is needed, the "show doctors" have time to make the necessary changes prior to the New York opening.

Test markets in a very real sense are the equivalent of taking the show on the road before opening in the Big Town. If the product is a total failure, loss of much money and corporate prestige is avoided. If there are problems but they are fixable, this can be accomplished quietly and with less disruption than if the problems were discovered after the full-blown national launch.

A test market provides valuable experience data on how customers react to your product. It is an opportunity to test several price points in paired comparison tests or several approaches to advertising or, less frequently, different packaging or different distribution systems.

If the test market is to include a TV advertising test, the markets to be tested must be chosen with great care. They must be relatively isolated geographically so that there is minimal media spillover from adjacent markets. In days past, it was relatively easy to pick test markets and we did not have to go far from major population centers. Such readily accessible cities as Albany, New York, Hartford, Connecticut, and Omaha, Nebraska, were fine for test market purposes.

The use of test markets, while they are still important and widely used, has been declining in popularity and in value as a predictive tool for at least a decade. There are at least four good reasons for this trend:

1. *Today, there are very few isolated or "pure" TV media markets with little or no spillover from nearby markets.* Whereas Albany, Hartford, and Springfield, Massachusetts, were fine test mar-

kets in years past, today one must go to more isolated places as Boise, Idaho, Sioux Falls, South Dakota, Spokane, Washington, or Augusta, Maine, to avoid media spillover from nearby major markets, and these isolated markets are not necessarily predictive of the rest of the country.

2. *The cost of even modest test markets has skyrocketed.* Today costs of $1 million to $2 million or more for a limited test market are not uncommon.

3. *The sophistication of competitors in learning about your test markets and doing their best to "muck them up" has grown exponentially.* Horror stories abound of the ingenious approaches devised by competitors to distort or destroy test market results.

4. *Perhaps most important, in many industries things just move too fast today to permit the luxury of six- to twelve-month test markets.* Test markets tip your hand to competition and give them valuable time to develop a knockoff that may be on the market by the time you have finished evaluating your test market.

Today product planners must often rely on a mixture of approaches that, taken together, will give them the feedback they need relative to new product market acceptance, faster and more accurately than the old-fashioned test market. In Chapter Twenty. I describe several creative approaches being used to replace or supplement the test market as a predictive device for new products.

# CHAPTER TWENTY

# Consumer Product
# Use Tests

In place of formal, structured test markets, which are expensive, lengthy, and highly subject to sabotage or disinformation techniques by competitors, more and more companies are turning to product placement tests and consumer usage tests.

Product placement tests are especially useful for home appliances and other consumer durables that are frequently used in the home. It is critical that the persons chosen to participate in these tests be representative in terms of demographics and life-style of the projected target market for the product.

Respondents may be asked to fill out a detailed questionnaire about their reactions to the product, or they may be asked to keep a diary for a period of one week or more detailing each incidence of their use of the product and their reactions to it.

Product placement tests can help a manufacturer determine the question of whether a new appliance, kitchen utensil, or other device is merely going to be purchased and put aside after a few trials or whether the product is going to have repeated use. In the former case, the product is really a novelty and a marketing program of high intensity but short duration is often indicated. When consumers are willing to make the behavior modification necessary to adopt a new product to their life-styles, that is a sign that the product will have a long life and that referrals and recommendations by satisfied users can be an important element in your market entry strategy.

Product placement tests are especially important for "razor/ razor blade" type products. For example, coffeemakers that use filters, VCRs that play cassettes, ice cream makers that use ingredients to make ice cream or yogurt, and vacuum cleaners that use disposable bags are all examples of razor/razor blade or hardware/software products where continued use rather than mere purchase is key to long-term success. In situations where sales of software, parts, ingredients, or "razor blades" over an extended period of time are critical to the success of the product, product use tests can be very helpful.

Consumer intercept tests, often conducted in shopping centers, are a method of performing one-time product usage tests or product taste tests on people who are representative of the likely target market.

Consumers are invited to visit immediately an on-site test center, either for a product taste test or a demonstration of a major new product. This is a fast and relatively inexpensive method of getting feedback on new products from prime prospects.

Consumer intercept tests are most useful for consumer package goods, including food, cosmetics, toiletries, where a one-time reaction is useful for product planning purposes.

Consumer test stores are a cost-effective method of testing consumer purchase behavior in a simulated shopping environment. Consumers are invited to a small test store, given an amount of money, and asked to select from among a variety of new products that are available for sale in the test market store. This approach can provide effective feedback relative to which products actually are selected in a simulated shopping environment.

Some would argue that these test store environments are artificial and do not truly replicate the real-life retail environment, and especially the environment of the large supermarket or massive department store, discount house, or catalog showroom in which the real purchase decision would most likely be made.

However, many companies find this to be an effective method of getting feedback on purchase reaction at a reasonable cost, prior to the full product launch.

# CHAPTER TWENTY-ONE

# Market Research on Industrial Products

The new product planning process in industrial goods companies is often driven by sales engineers or the engineering department and, in the larger companies, by the R&D department. New product development time is lengthy, often three years or longer, and the number of new product development projects that can be undertaken is often quite limited. Thus, good market research on new products can be critical to the success and survival of the company.

The type of research most appropriate for industrial products is often the in-depth personal interview conducted by an experienced marketing consultant with the purchasing agents, the user department, or the design engineering people of major prospective purchasers.

One continuing concern with industrial products market research is that the sample size is often thought to be too small to be statistically accurate or projectable to the universe of your customers.

In fact, when conducting industrial research the critical issue is not what percentage of your customers is surveyed, but rather, what percentage of your present or potential sales volume for the product in question is accounted for by survey respondents.

In a large majority of industrial market research situations, the 80/20 rule applies (in some cases it is more like a 90/10 rule) where 20 percent of the customers account for 80 percent of sales volume. When a small number of customers account for a large percentage of your sales, it is critical that all or most of these big customers be included in the survey.

It is also important to segment or stratify the sample by end-use application or by the industry group of the customer or by whatever relevant variable that is likely to influence reaction to the new product or overall purchase behavior.

For example, customers who tend to be conservative in their own business approach are less likely to be prime prospects for your new product in its early stages of market introduction.

For complex industrial products where a number of people at the prospect company get involved in the purchase decision, it is necessary to interview a number of different people. It is especially important to touch base both with the people who appraise new products, those who write specifications upon which new products are judged and accepted, and most important, the end users of the product as well as the purchasing people who qualify and negotiate with suppliers.

Usually, all of these people are knowledgeable and keenly interested in new products that are responsive to their needs. In most cases, they are accessible and will provide valuable insights into the merits of the proposed features and benefits of the new product from the vantage point of the customer. Industrial customers can usually provide the necessary inputs working off a product concept statement. Sometimes a mockup of the product or a detailed set of specifications will be necessary.

But in all cases the interviewer must be knowledgeable about the products and markets in question. These research interviews are best conducted as discussions between knowledgeable professionals and not as a stereotyped question and answer session between interviewer and respondent.

One danger of this kind of market research will be the "it depends" syndrome. Typically, industrial research respondents often qualify their reactions to the product and their willingness to purchase it on the ability of the product to meet certain performance standards, often over a period of time, at a given price level. For this research to be meaningful, the interviewer must propose specific scenarios and force respondents to commit themselves regarding their purchase behavior in specific situations.

Many industrial goods companies attempt to use their salespeople, reps, or agents to conduct this kind of product research, if indeed they do it at all. I would argue that market research is often not the best use of time for high-level sales engineers. More important, the skills required to conduct an effective in-depth market research interview and those required to sell the product are quite different. In our experience, executive salespeople don't like to do research, and often don't do it very well. This is especially true when they are paid in whole or in part or commission based on volume of sales generated.

# CHAPTER TWENTY-TWO

# Pricing Research

Often the most difficult question on which to get accurate feedback is the critical question, "How much will you pay for the product?"

Information relative to pricing is usually an integral part of the market research survey, whichever survey methodology is employed.

Often feedback on price sensitivity and customer reactions to specific price points is the single most important topic to be covered and the prime reason the research is conducted in the first place.

However, it is usually advisable to "low key" the price research component. In most cases this subject should be covered at or near the end of the survey, when rapport has been established with the respondent and he or she is reasonably familiar with the values, features, and benefits of the new product or service.

A complete treatment of the various techniques of developing price parameters and estimating price sensitivity would require a large book all by itself. Here my purpose is more limited. It is to discuss some of the applications and the limitations of pricing research, some approaches that may yield contradictory or inaccurate data as well as those that help to identify the specific values and applications of various types of pricing research.

Here, suffice it to say that a properly structured survey research instrument is usually able to accomplish one or more of the following limited objectives:

- *Determine the acceptable range of pricing.* The highest acceptable price, the modal or most frequently quoted price, and the lowest price that will optimize unit sales with acceptable levels of profit can often be obtained. Prospects are often able to give a range of reasonable prices that they would consider but often are not sure of their own purchase decision at a set price point.

Such questions as the following can often yield useful price parameters:

"What is the highest price you would consider paying for this product?"
"At what price would you expect to see this product being sold at your local supermarket/department store?"

- *Provide a rough measure of price sensitivity.* A reasonable estimate of total unit sales at three or more price points that correspond to a high middle, and low pricing strategy can sometimes be accomplished.

In this case you would ask potential customers to provide estimates of purchase volume, purchase frequency, or likelihood of purchase at three or more price points.

- *Indicate that for many products, the "numbers just don't work."* In most cases, this means that the sales volume at your proposed price will be too low or the price at which you can sell your necessary breakeven number of units will be too low for the product to reach breakeven or to make money any time in the foreseeable future.

This is often the most valuable application of pricing research. It is often a fast and inexpensive way of demonstrating that the pet idea of a powerful person, key customer, or whoever is just not viable in the marketplace.

There are certain caveats to pricing research that must be observed by anyone attempting to do this work.

First, focus groups are often not the most effective forum for dealing with pricing issues.

Second, there is often much bias inherent in the answers to the pricing question. The skill of the survey designer in structuring questions to minimize the bias factor and to provide consistency checks is essential.

Third, recognize that even when no bias factor is present, people confronted with making a pricing decision for a product that only exists on paper are only giving you their best guess as to what they really will do when the real product hits the market. But even customer feedback that is only 75 percent accurate is usually better than the "guesstimates" of the product planner.

# Mini-Histories

# 19

## Chemical Tank Trailer Cleaning Service

### "What If We Gave a Party and Nobody Came?"

In 1979, a major chemical company saw an opportunity for applying its technology to chemical tank trailer cleaning. Management became very excited about this business, seeing it as a whole new service area for the company. In 1980, the company committed itself to building a plant for tank trailer cleaning.

In April 1981, the company opened the new plant and invited tank trailer owners to have their units cleaned for an introductory cost of $1 per trailer. Many came, and the company was able to clean over two-thirds of them. In June 1981, it started commercial pricing—at a base price of about $250 per trailer. Instead of the anticipated ten to thirty trailers per day (three hundred to nine hundred per month), only twenty-three trailers came for the *whole month of June.* And they were all tough products to clean. By 1982, the company had closed the plant.

What went wrong? Why, when a profitable, well-managed large company had anticipated a rate of ten to thirty trailers per day—at least three hundred per month—did fewer than thirty a month show up? What made this "exciting idea" a total new product Loser in the real world?

This was a classic case of the "solution in search of a problem." Because company management was entranced with the technology and saw this as a whole new business field to conquer, it did not adequately analyze the market factors. Management heard "that would be nice" in their research and wrongly interpreted that as "I'll pay for that." They saw developing governmental regulations and interpreted those as establishing their new service requirements without thinking of the possible results of very lax or limited enforcement of the actual regulations by the government. And, because they were so eager to go forward, they later found the cost was 50 percent higher than the initial forecasts.

What did the market really say? It said four things that the company surely could have discovered before building the plant rather than after:

- Price is the dominant factor in selecting the chemical tank trailer cleaner.
- The chemical tank trailer cleaning business is strongly affected by both the local and national regulatory and enforcement climate (but regulation was not seen at that time as a problem).
- Tank trailer cleaning was viewed as "manageable" by most prospects.
- Available tank trailer cleaning services, with an average cost of about $100 per trailer, were adequate to industry needs.

## Key Lesson

Check the market before you spend the hard cash to build the plant and produce the product. Talk to real customers, not just government bureaucrats. Apply common sense and tests of reasonableness to the market information. Don't get blinded by technical elegance. Otherwise you may give a party and find that nobody comes.

—*George Seiler*

# 20

## Oil of Olay

### Hang in There, Baby!

In the early 1970s, Richardson-Vicks USA acquired a small company in Florida that formulated and marketed a cosmetic cream called Oil of Olay. Made partly from aloe, the product was positioned against mature women (35 and over) as a wrinkle softener, antiaging cosmetic.

Early sales were disappointing and some of the product managers at Richardson-Vicks were convinced the package design and color, inherited from the former owners, were not right for the product. Our assignment was to conduct a research study and market analysis to determine the fate of Oil of Olay.

Interviews with department store buyers and merchandising managers indicated that distribution and in-store merchandising for Oil of Olay were weak but that the product, and especially its off-key and therefore memorable package and name, had potential in the marketplace.

The dominant product in the category, at the time, was called Second Debut. This product had a strong market share but was not highly rated by merchandise managers for its product quality, in-store merchandising, or profit margin. A great name and excellent advertising theme were the perceived strengths of Second Debut.

Our advice to the client was to hang tough with Oil of Olay—don't change the formula, certainly don't change the package, but develop a new advertising positioning and start heavy in-store merchandising in the leading department stores in major cities.

Over a fifteen-year period, Second Debut faded and Oil of Olay blossomed. So did the product niche category as demographic shifts and life-style preferences brought major increases in the number of women buying antiaging cosmetics. Richardson-Vicks also skillfully extended the Oil of Olay concept from a stand-alone product to a short line of specialized cosmetics, all utilizing the Oil of Olay name and the classic package design. As noted by Michael Porter in his classic, *Competitive Advantage*, Oil of Olay also consolidated its lead by broadening distribution into the supermarket channel when this market niche had grown to sufficient size to require wider distribution. An analysis of this product in *The New York Times* Business Section in 1986 noted the Oil of Olay line had generated after-tax profits of $35 million for Richardson-Vicks in the previous year.

So because it believed the research and was not locked in to its first impressions, Richardson-Vicks was rewarded with a Big Winner in Oil of Olay.

## Key Lesson

A modest investment in professional marketing research to get an objective outside "second opinion" before deciding to terminate a product line or an acquisition is usually prudent. The cost is very small compared to the potential benefits. The Oil of Olay story illustrates three critical success factors in new product introductions:

1. Don't be discouraged by early failure—check out the nature of the problem via research and fix it.
2. Build a complementary line of products around your base product.
3. If your product appeals to an age group, look at the demographics five to ten years out and determine to what extent that age group will grow in those five to ten years.

Even a cursory look at the U.S. age mix will tell you that the 76 million baby boomers, born between 1946 and 1964, will make the mature market the dominant market of the early twenty-first century.

# 21

## Goulds' Process Pumps

## The Customer Is Our Ally, Not Our "Friendly Competitors"

Goulds' Pumps produces centrifugal process pumps. It had been successful in many water-pumping applications and had profitably targeted specific market segments in the chemical and petroleum process industries. Goulds' saw the pulp and paper industry as a potentially attractive process pump market segment and decided to tackle this market.

Three major equipment manufacturers had long dominated the sale of process pumps to the pulp and paper industry. They had set up their businesses and marketing approaches to supply customers without competing aggressively, staying friendly with one another and treating their selling and marketing efforts as a "gentlemen's game"—in other words, a classic oligopoly situation. They organized along product lines so that new pumps and spare parts and service were separate organizations. They supplied quality products, but the companies themselves were difficult to deal with. Both service and delivery were judged slow by the market.

The Goulds' management team researched the pulp and paper companies' objectives. They discovered that these companies looked for new pumps for major projects at relatively low cost.

Goulds' devised the following overall strategy:

- Price new units to get them in place.
- Be user friendly and easy to deal with, compared to the "three friendly oligopolists."
- Support customers with excellent service and parts.

Goulds' bought its way into new accounts via low initial prices and then made its profit on the parts and service business.

138

By recognizing both the customers' objectives and the competitors' complacency, Goulds' Pumps became the major pump supplier in this market.

This product line extension, to a great extent offering existing products in a new market segment, has been a Big Winner for Goulds'.

## Key Lessons

The Goulds' success was based on a combination of factors, not the least of which is the application of the four basic questions (noted in Chapter Seven) that should be answered each time a market or product strategy is under consideration:

1. Who is our customer?
2. What does the customer buy?
3. What is value to the customer?
4. How can we gain competitive advantage?

In looking to gain competitive advantage, the Goulds people also asked, "How can we change the rules of the game in our favor?" Here competitor complacency opened the door for a major market/product opportunity.

—*George Seiler*

# 22

## Pampers

## Changing the Way We Change the Baby

If Pringles represents the occasional gaffe of a great company, the introduction and market buildup of Pampers shows Procter & Gamble at the top of its game.

In the mid-1960s, my firm was retained to conduct a market analysis by a trade association called the Diaper Service Industries of America. This trade group represented the hundreds of local companies who performed the task of picking up a weekly load of used cloth diapers and delivering a fresh supply to the consumer's home each week.

After growing and flourishing for many years, this service was suddenly devastated by a newfangled contraption called the disposable diaper, which was being marketed directly to mothers through supermarkets and drugstores.

This new product worked so well and provided so many benefits and conveniences that the game was pretty well over for the diaper services. Disposables were softer, reduced diaper rash, and were an aesthetically superior way to deal with this necessary task of child raising.

A breakthrough product that was a Big Winner from the start, the market introduction of Pampers was based on solid research and a strong advertising program. Most important, Pampers hit the market in that mid-1960s period when many women were redefining their roles and looking for such life-style and time-saving improvements that would permit them to balance the roles of mother, working woman, and wife. And the switch to Pampers helped many women to manage this life-style change.

A superior sales force, a consistently high level of quality, and a splendid logistics and physical distribution system have enabled Pampers to build and hold a dominant market share, successfully fighting off competition from LUVS, Kimbies, and even Johnson & Johnson.

The diaper services are now attempting to make a come-back based on environmental concerns connected with disposable diapers. However, as of early 1990, the market share of the diaper services stood at 10 percent, while disposables held 90 percent of the market.

## Key Lesson

A major breakthrough product, which has very real advantages over the product currently used, is most likely going to be a success in any event. But this success will be enhanced if the breakthrough product's introduction coincides with life-style changes that make it even more attractive to the target market.

Procter & Gamble has a strong market research/analysis capability to complement their fabled product management expertise. The timing of the introduction of Pampers was based on solid demographic and life-style research, not serendipity.

# 23

## Perrier

## The Blockbuster Product From the Center of the Earth

At the turn of the decade, it is appropriate to select the outstanding new product introduction of the 1980s. Many advertising and marketing people have argued that this honor belongs not to one of the marvelous consumer electronics products or one of the many biotechnology breakthroughs, but rather to a simple green bottle of bubbling water that calls itself "the earth's first soft drink."

Much has been written about the rise of Perrier to a 35 percent market share in the high-growth category of bottled mineral waters. Many reasons have been advanced for the breathtaking success of Perrier, and all of them have some degree of truth—a truly fresh and superior flavor, the beautifully shaped green bottle, a brilliant but low-key advertising program, the name Perrier, an energetic and entrepreneurial American distributor, and so on and so forth.

However, it seemed that these answers missed something of the underlying reason for the great status or snob appeal of Perrier—its ability to get people to willingly pay an upcharge for one brand of bubbly water over another. Discussions with several restaurateur colleagues, close observers of the human scene, added the missing element in the analysis, which goes as follows:

Hundreds of thousands of salespeople, account executives, and entrepreneurs must entertain customers, prospects, and clients at lunch every day. For decades, it was considered de rigueur for both salesman and client to quaff a social drink or two or three as part of this business lunch. As concern with health matters rose and the need for salespeople and executive productivity in the afternoon rose with it, more and more salespeople and customers wanted to move to an alcohol-free lunch. Light beer and white wine helped somewhat but didn't really solve the problem. And to abstain totally often sent the message to your dining companion that one was a bluenose abstainer or a recovering alcoholic.

Then, just as these life-style currents were becoming felt, along came this wonderful new mineral water that said in many ways that "it's chic not to drink booze at lunch!" The great success of Perrier also has to do with its timing. People were ready, willing, and eager to find a credible reason that enabled them to pass up alcohol without losing prestige in the eyes of their luncheon companions. And Perrier gave them that reason.

## Key Lesson

The moral is that for some product introductions the state of the life-style and values of the prospect market can be a key to success. Some products like the VCR change life-styles; some, like Perrier, ride these life-style changes to great success. A Big Winner in every respect, Perrier proves that not only break-through products but even very mundane products, brilliantly planned and introduced, can achieve great success in the marketplace.

## Postscript

The product recall announced by Perrier in the spring of 1990 pulled this product off the market for about ten weeks. Some analysts speculate that Perrier will lose market share and perhaps its market dominance because of this window of opportunity provided to its competitors. I am betting on Perrier. The integrity and professionalism with which they handled the recall, and a $25 million advertising reentry budget, should enable them to hold the top position.

## Winning Ideas

1. In the final analysis, the reaction of the consumer is the acid test for a new product introduction. Amazingly, many companies, because of arrogance, ignorance, or to "save money," fail to get valuable advance consumer feedback on the new products.
2. Life-style and demographic research is critical for nearly all consumer products. The role that the new product will play in the life-style of customers, and the extent to which it will improve their lives and save time, money, or hassle, needs to be factored into your product planning.
3. Both consumer markets and industrial goods markets can be profitably segmented in ways that will assist you to focus in your market introduction plan on the most likely early purchasers of the new product. Market segmentation techniques range from a simple ordering of customers in a time priority to the use of sophisticated computer-based demographics systems.
4. It is essential that the proper research technique be chosen, the proper questions asked, and that an appropriate sample of potential users be contacted. Most important, this work needs to be accomplished by professionals, not as a side assignment for your sales force.
5. Focus groups have application at the product concept stage before a serious investment is made in product planning or R&D. Focus groups are most useful for breakthrough products and for product concepts that are new or that require in-depth analysis of the customer's reaction to the product or service.
6. The Delphi research technique is an iterative process that utilizes the talents of experts and industry gurus to evaluate products and concepts where the target customer lacks the experience to make an informed judgment.
7. Test markets are expensive and time consuming and subject to sabotage by your competitors, but a well-orchestrated test market can be insurance against disaster in a major new product introduction.

8. Consumer use tests are increasingly being used in place of test markets, since they are cheaper, faster, and more likely to preserve the confidentiality of the project.

9. Research on industrial and high-technology products should be conducted by marketing professionals who have the appropriate technical background. Here sample size is less important, but you must get accurate feedback from large and important customers.

10. For almost every new product introduction, it is important to segment customers into two or more groups that have different needs, motivations, or purchase patterns. The accompanying figure sums up the various types of new product market research and their applications.

## Primary Applications for Various Types of New Product Market Research

**Focus groups:**
- Provide early input to product development people for:
  —Designing breakthrough products
  —Identifying new markets for established products
  —Helping to segment the market

**Delphi panels:**
- Used when consensus forecasts are needed
  —Time-consuming; requires highly skilled project manager
- Provide expert input for:
  —Qualitative or policy issues
  —Macro, long-term, or technical research trends

**Consumer product placement or use:**
- Tests receptivity and reflects actual usage
- Will spot a bad product idea quickly
- Not always reliable for pricing purposes
- Careful sample selection and adequate incentives to participants essential
- Product test diaries must be complete and accurately filled out

**Industrial product market research:**
- Provides valuable technical input to product planning
- Requires professional consultants
- Must weigh responses based on purchasing potential of each respondent
- Small samples often not projectable to total market potential

**Pricing research:**
- More useful in determining upper and lower range of acceptable pricing than in setting exact price
- Potential for bias, self-serving answers very high
- Need devices that reduce bias factor

**Market segmentation:**
- Useful in designing product promotional strategies
- Expensive, time-consuming
- Requires expert practitioner to design study and analyze results
- Requires a clearcut concept of how results will be used before authorizing market segmentation

# SECTION IV

# PLANNING FOR NEW PRODUCTS IN DIFFERENT KINDS OF COMPANIES

Success in bringing new products to market depends on your ability to custom-craft your new product planning system and your new product introduction and delivery system to the specific needs of your company and business situation.

As has been noted, there is no one magic "cookie cutter" product planning system that will work for all companies, or even for all companies in a given size range or in a particular industry.

This section analyzes the critical variables and the critical success factors that you must consider for particular kinds of companies, products, and industries.

# CHAPTER TWENTY-THREE

# New Products in Startup Companies

Thousands of companies have started on the thrust of break-through new products. Many images came to mind—Steve Jobs and Steve Wozniak building the first Apple computer, Bill Gates developing his software at Microsoft, Clarence Birdseye perfecting the first flash-frozen foods, "Colonel" Harlan Sanders concocting the formula for his Kentucky Fried Chicken, and so on. The startup company had a renaissance in the late 1970s and early 1980s, primarily in high-tech industries.

However, while startup companies have provided a spark to our economy, there have also been a number of major failures. People Express, for example, enjoyed spectacular growth for some years only to come totally unglued because of failure to develop the support systems and infrastructure needed to support its growth. As we enter the 1990s, the concept of the startup company, even in glamourous high-tech fields, has lost some of its allure for venture capitalists and other sources of seed capital for startups. This is doubly true when the new product that is the basis and rationale for the startup company is itself new and untested in the marketplace.

The basic statistics of startup companies are frightening at first glance. Fully 80 percent of all startup companies fail and have disappeared within five years of their startup date. Yet closer analysis reveals that, in the small minority of cases where the three key variables discussed below are met, the *success* rate for startup companies and their new products is 80 percent or better.

The three critical success factors must *all* be present for the 80 percent or better success formula for startups to apply. Incidentally, success is defined as still being in business five years from the startup day. These three critical success factors are:

1. *The founder(s) of the company has a thorough knowledge of the business he or she starting—knowledge based on recent past experience.* Having achieved a strong track record of success in the same or a closely related product category in the recent past will be a strong plus. The world, especially the world of customers, trade press, and venture capitalists must be made aware of this track record of success. It doesn't help if you were really the genius behind a great new product, if the world thinks it was your boss or three other people who were responsible for this success.

Without this track record of success and past accomplishment in the same or a closely related business, the avenue of venture capital or bank loans will be *totally* closed to the new startup entrepreneur, no ifs, ands, or buts.

2. *The founder(s) has adequate financing, generated from his or her own funds or from friends and true believers, to support him/herself and to fund the business for the first six to twelve months.* Even the fledgling entrepreneur who has a track record of success in the business very often finds that banks and venture capitalists will not touch him or her until the business has been established, even in a laboratory or pilot mode, and the first few sales have been made and the first few customers obtained.

The startup entrepreneur must be prepared to provide the basic startup equity needed to launch the business. Often this requires such measures as using home equity or second mortgages, borrowing against life insurance, investing the payout from an employment contract, and other variants of "betting the farm" on the new product and the startup venture.

In addition, the founder must be prepared to invest

"sweat equity," consisting of eighty- and ninety-hour work weeks during which he or she draws no salary, often for six months to a year, until the cash flow turns positive.

However, this willingness of the entrepreneur to bet the farm and put in the sweat equity tells us two important things. First, the entrepreneur truly believes in the value of the product or service and in the future of the company. Second, the entrepreneur is personally 100 percent committed to its success and willing to make whatever personal sacrifice is necessary to "make it happen."

3. *The founder has a detailed, professionally prepared business plan on paper, including a market analysis and a market introduction plan, and a cash flow projection for the products or services he or she plans to offer to the market.* All too often, the startup entepreneur resists the mental discipline of preparing a business plan—or worse yet, views the business plan merely as a necessary evil whose sole purpose is to persuade bankers, friends, or venture capitalists to supply the necessary seed capital. This type of founder strongly resists the concept of the business plan as the basic control document for managing the new business. Needless to say, entrepreneurs who operate with this mindset almost invariably join the ranks of the 80 percent who do not celebrate the fifth anniversary of their business startup.

When one or more of these three critical success elements are lacking, the *failure* rate of the startup business is in the 95 percent plus range. When all three of the key success ingredients are present, the *success* rate (defined as still being in business five years from the startup date) is in the 80 percent or better range.

## The Twofold Challenge

The startup entrepreneur has a twofold challenge. He or she must do the right things to firmly establish a company, while going through the steps necessary to bring a new product to market successfully.

Here's some advice for the startup entrepreneur:

1. *Concentrate on the new product.* A critical success factor

**Figure 23-1.** Success and failure.

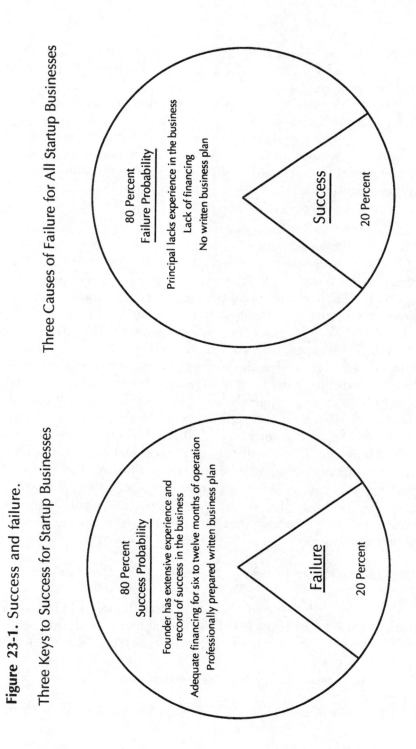

Three Keys to Success for Startup Businesses

Three Causes of Failure for All Startup Businesses

80 Percent
Success Probability

Founder has extensive experience and
record of success in the business
Adequate financing for six to twelve months of operation
Professionally prepared written business plan

Failure

20 Percent

80 Percent
Failure Probability

Principal lacks experience in the business
Lack of financing
No written business plan

Success

20 Percent

for the startup company is the self-discipline of the founder to focus almost all of his or her energies on developing and perfecting the product, getting the manufacturing and service capabilities established, and preparing and executing the market entry strategy.

2. *Delegate the company startup issues to competent specialists.* There are a number of critical activities, none of them insignificant, that must be accomplished in the course of establishing a new company. These include:

- Locating a suitable office and production facility
- Hiring employees or farming out work to subcontractors
- Retaining lawyers, accountants, or management or marketing consultants to render necessary services in their areas of expertise
- Negotiating with banks and other sources of financing
- Establishing the systems and procedures, operational and financial controls necessary to run the business

Typically, the successful entrepreneur is heavily involved with the product and the market and may relate only peripherally to these critical administrative and organizational issues. If the entrepreneur is really a promoter, who is primarily involved with starting companies but who does not really know "in his or her bones" the products or services the company will provide, disaster is almost certain.

The ability to recruit and retain a strong, honest, hardworking, well-balanced person to handle the administrative and financial issues listed above permits the entrepreneur to concentrate on product development, marketing, and manufacturing. The specific mix of responsibilities between "Mr. Outside" and "Ms. Inside" varies based on the specific talents and experience each brings to the venture. Most important of all is the chemistry, trust, and respect that exist between them.

Often taking this inside/outside path means giving up some valuable equity and delegation of some major responsibilities to Mr. or Ms. Inside. But this is often the critical success factor for the startup company.

Figure 23-1 sums up key ideas presented in this chapter.

# CHAPTER TWENTY-FOUR

# New Products in Entrepreneurial Companies

The established but still small and usually entrepreneurial company has a different set of critical success factors in bringing new products to market.

As in the startup company, the hands-on, close, and continuing involvement of the entrepreneur in the processes of new product and marketing planning is essential. But now there is an ongoing business that must be managed as well. Most successful entrepreneurial companies run "lean and mean." A fully dedicated product planning team is a luxury they cannot afford.

When it is time to develop a major new product or to perfect the new, improved, next-generation product (or service) that will be necessary for the company to continue its growth, invariably the founder will be the product champion, and will be heavily involved in developing this new product.

The critical variable often in short supply is competent, dedicated second-level management that is capable of managing key operations such as sales and manufacturing, freeing up the entrepreneur to focus on developing new products and building the business.

Entrepreneurial companies have some built-in advantages over their larger rivals when it comes to developing and perfecting new products. New products generally go through the product development process much faster and for a fraction of the cost, in smaller or entrepreneurial companies, than they do in the typical large, complex company.

Fewer memos are written, there are fewer committees, the committees have fewer members, and most of the key participants in the product planning process are too busy with their full-time jobs to get involved in the kind of political in-fighting that so often slows down and sometimes derails good product ideas in big companies.

Above all, the active role of the founder CEO in the product development process tends to keep everyone focused and motivated, and helps to cut through the various delays and roadblocks that can slow up the product development process.

But there are offsets to the advantages enjoyed by lean, mean entrepreneurial companies in developing new products.

The entrepreneurial company, being resource constrained and cash poor, often subcontracts out critical elements in the process or must depend on the technology, expertise, and time schedule of outside suppliers or companies not under their control. This adds to the danger that a new product introduction will fail to meet its target date or that it will have a defect in technology, design, or whatever that must be corrected prior to introduction.

Perhaps more than other companies, the entrepreneurial company must be on guard against the "bad idea with a powerful champion." As noted, the product champion in the entrepreneurial company is likely to be the CEO him or herself. It is very difficult for many employees to tell a dynamic, creative, often brilliant, genius inventor boss that this one particular idea is a "bummer."

A critical success factor for the entrepreneurial company relative to bringing new products to market is the willingness to invest some modest resources in market research and in having the mature business judgment to change items such as product specs, pricing, market entry strategy, or market positioning, when necessary, based on this research.

It is a long accepted maxim that "real entrepreneurs don't do market research." Even *Inc. Magazine*, which regularly sings the praises of the entrepreneur, has felt it necessary from time to time to remind their entrepreneur readers of the values of market research and business planning.

In reality, the entrepreneur is often so emotionally involved with the new product that he or she does not want to hear any negative feedback from the market. What the entrepreneur misses, however, are the fine-tuning adjustments and refinements that, when added by knowledgeable customers, can often spell the difference between acceptance or rejection of the new product by the market.

So the challenge in a small entrepreneurial company is the establishment of a workable review process for new product planning and a reasonable set of financial controls and disciplines. I submit that the best time to do this is not when the inventor/entrepreneur boss is infatuated with a great new idea, but rather during the less stressful periods when the issue of establishing an organized new product planning process can be discussed in a professional, nonemotional, nonthreatening manner.

An entrepreneur who recognizes the need to use key executives as a genuine advisory group, rather than merely as robots to implement the grand design, is likely to have a much higher success rate with new product introductions than an entrepreneur who does not. Most important, such an entrepreneur averts the kind of megabomb product introduction that can and all too often does sink the small, entrepreneurial company.

# CHAPTER TWENTY-FIVE

# New Products in Large, Complex Companies

Nearly all of the textbooks, seminars, and articles that deal with new product planning, product development, and marketing are oriented toward large, complex, multiproduct, multidivisional (usually bureaucratic) companies. Yet in spite of all this body of literature and the earnest efforts of many dedicated professionals, it usually takes three times as long, requires three times as many people, and costs three times as much money for the large company to bring a new product to market than it does for the small company.

Richard T. Pascale in his book *Managing on the Edge* (Simon & Schuster, 1990, p. 46) notes that a National Science Foundation study conducted in 1984 found that for each R&D dollar expended, small firms achieved *four times* as many innovations as did medium-size firms and they achieved an incredible *twenty-four times* as many innovations per R&D dollar as did large firms.

In many large, complex firms, *the process is the problem.* There are some new products for which the standard new product planning process is too slow or that will either abort a product that should reach the market or permit a product that is going to be a Loser to hit the market.

There are some excellent textbooks and articles on the subject of product management (see Appendix C) that provide various organization charts and suggested operating systems for the product development process in large companies. Rather than duplicate these efforts, we will focus on a few simple and hopefully workable approaches that, when followed, will result in dramatic improvement in the cost effectiveness and market response time of the new product development process in many large, complex companies.

1. *Keep the product planning and product development team lean, mean, and very professional.* Reduce the number of casual onlookers. When specialists are needed for a particular expertise bring them in for "cameo roles" as needed, but don't have them as regular members of the team.

2. *Offer employment contracts of three to five years' duration to all key people in the new product planning, development, and marketing process.* This policy accomplishes the following objectives.

It removes the fear of failure which is often an impediment to the kind of creativity and entrepreneurial spirit needed to succeed at new products, especially in large bureaucratic companies.

It acts to depoliticize the environment of the product planning process. People with contracts can freely speak their minds against a bad idea without fear of losing their jobs.

Also, the reaction of the key employee to the offer of a contract will speak volumes about his or her level of commitment to the company as opposed to the commitment to their profession or specialty. My experience with Japanese companies (see Chapter Twenty-Eight) has convinced me that you are best advised to entrust the future of your company to people whose primary loyalty and orientation is to *your company* and not to their own particular skill set.

The contract separates the company people who will provide valuable service for years to come from those who are merely passing through.

Employees do not usually break employment contracts. However, they cannot be forced to sign. Those who decline to sign can still be employed in nonsensitive situations, but do not count on them for your product development process over the long term.

3. *Staff your product planning team with people with a genuine feel and, yes, a love for the product category. This is critical to the success of new product planning.* Professional product managers, generally MBAs who have excellent analytical capabilities, indeed have a role to play. But unless they are really "into the product," use them for their strengths in research, analysis, systems, and organization, while the "true believers" work on the bone and marrow of new product development.

As more and more companies beyond the large consumer packaged goods companies adopt the product manager concept, they find that "hands-on" experience with the product is more critical than the specific analytical and marketing disciplines associated with the product management function. These functional skills can be acquired through seminars and personalized self-development and training courses more readily than one can acquire a feel for a business and a love for the product.

4. *Don't overuse the task force approach and be very careful in using matrix management.* Special new product task forces should be reserved for major breakthrough products which require special handling apart from the basic new product development process. To set up special interdepartmental task forces to deal with the ordinary run of line extension products and new, improved, next-generation products is to trivialize the task force concept and strip it of its urgency.

Matrix management, an elaborate and sophisticated theory, works well in the real world only in very specialized situations.

The Bible tells us that "a man cannot serve two masters." Experience indicates that the biblical maxim also applies to business organization and especially to the art of bringing new products to market. The matrix management concept sounds good in seminars and looks good on organization charts, but it rarely helps to move things along to meet the target introduction date.

5. *Require a quarterly in-depth review of all new product development projects, with all senior management in attendance.* These

meetings can be brief, and should be supplemented by monthly progress reports to senior management. This quarterly review should be based on an agreed-on format and should deal frankly and honestly with the unsolved challenges as well as the progress already achieved.

Critical to this review process is total honesty on the part of the project people doing the presenting and total support for their efforts on the part of the top management review team.

Review sessions where the continued funding of the project is contingent on making a high-powered presentation to skeptical senior managers are all too often the norm in companies that "manage by the numbers." They are also a good prescription for ensuring a new product development process that works far below its potential.

6. *Clearly define the special roles of various key departments—R&D, product development, engineering, marketing, and staff support services—in the new product development process in a written document.* As noted in Chapter Seven, a separate section in the business plan should be devoted to new products. This is an appropriate place for such a policy statement and for defining the role and the expected contribution of all key units in the company to the new product introduction process.

7. *Every three to five years, retain a qualified management consultant to perform a management audit of the new product development process and of its results.* There are a number of Association of Management Consulting Firms (ACME, Inc.) that are very well qualified to perform this kind of assignment. In addition, some individual Certified Management Consultants have the credentials to do this work. Recently retired executives and others who combine both broad business experience, strong analytical skills, and a knowledge of your industry can also be used to perform the new product planning audit.

The management audit should be low-key, nonthreatening, and oriented toward constructive suggestions to improve future performance rather than to assigning blame for any past failures.

The audit should provide answers to the following key questions:

- Is the mandate for new products clear, and do all key people know what their responsibilities are relative to new products?
- How do new product ideas get generated, appraised, and acted on? Is the process open or closed?
- Is there any follow-up mechanism to ensure that each new product idea submitted receives competent review before being dismissed?
- How detailed are the project plans for new products?
- What monitoring mechanisms are in place to assure that the new product plan is on target?
- What procedures exist to permit specific new product development projects to bypass the system to accelerate their market development?
- How is the effectiveness of the new product development process judged, by what standards, and by whom?
- How do we determine if the best-qualified people are actually being deployed on the most important new product development projects?

To the greatest extent practicable, this audit should be quantitative as well as qualitative. The use of rating scales and similar devices, consistently and honestly applied, will permit a benchmark to be established against which future progress can be measured.

# CHAPTER TWENTY-SIX

# New Products in Consumer Package Goods Companies

A *consumer package good* is defined as follows: A consumer package goods product usually sells for less than $20, is eaten, drunk, or applied to the body, comes in a very attractive package, is sold in a supermarket or drugstore, and relies heavily on advertising and in-store positioning and display. Most important, the store salesperson's role in the product or brand selection process is often minimal.

Consumer package goods account for a sizable majority of the 10,000 plus new products that reach the market in the United States each year. Not surprisingly, consumer package goods companies often devote a higher percentage of their resources, and relatively more of their best and brightest marketing people, to the new product introduction process than do most companies in other industry categories.

In spite of this, the success and failure rate of the large consumer package goods companies is not appreciably better than those of companies less sophisticated in marketing.

There are two reasons for this:

1. Competition for shelf space in the supermarket, the

discount house, the drugstore, and other retail chains grows more intense each day. The store does not expand its shelf space to display your new product. The battle for retail shelf space is the ultimate win/lose game.

2. All too many new consumer package goods products offer no tangible benefit and often only the scantest psychic benefit or convenience over products already on the market.

To put it bluntly, in some mature product categories there are too many new consumer package goods products. They only serve to confuse the consumer, who already has too many items in the product category to deal with. The new package goods product sometimes appeals to a very specialized segment of the market that may exist primarily in the mind of the product manager or in the fertile imagination of the advertising copywriter.

In bringing new consumer packaged products to market, the critical success factors, all of which must be addressed in the product planning process, are the three *Ps*—Product, Packaging, and Positioning.

## Product

As noted, consumer package goods account for over two-thirds of the ten thousand-plus new products introduced to the market each year. While some are genuine breakthrough products, often what is "new" is very minor indeed. Many new consumer products merely add one ingredient, or provide an established product in a new flavor, new package, or size. Sometimes these small differences meet a need and are accepted, but often the total market is not expanded.

## Packaging

The packaging including the design and configuration of the package, and the name of the product are critical to its success. A well-organized consumer package goods product development operation gives equal or greater weight, time, and effort to packaging as to formulation of the product itself. In such product categories as cosmetics, it is not uncommon for the cost of the packaging to equal or exceed the cost of raw ingredients of the product.

## Positioning

A new product can be a mass market item, which is given strong advertising support and marketing effort, and is sold in volume to the mass market. The other option is the specialty niche product, precisely targeted to a preselected group of consumers who have a specific need or interest. This can be an age group, income group, special interest group, ethnic group, or a product that appeals to people with a specific life-style.

There is no middle ground in the fiercely competitive world of consumer package goods marketing. The *stuck-in-the-middle product,* which cannot generate the power marketing muscle necessary to compete in the mass market, but which lacks the specific unique feature or benefit necessary to make it a niche product, is a guaranteed stone loser.

Whatever the case, the planning for the niche market product especially must be intensive, and must include professional market research. Precise definition of the niche is essential, as are sharply targeted communications, including the advertising and the product promotion programs.

The new product development group should and usually does devote as much time, money, and talent to the positioning of the product as they do to formulating the product and designing the package.

All too often the positioning of a new product is thought to relate specifically to the advertising message that is conveyed in print, radio, or TV to the target market. But the positioning of the product, to be truly professional and totally effective, must be approached holistically. The positioning of a product, properly defined, includes all the elements of the marketing mix which taken together convey the message and the value of the product to its target market.

# CHAPTER TWENTY-SEVEN

# New Products in Consumer Durable Goods Companies

While consumer package goods are truly consumed, consumer durables are characterized by a long life. Typically, they come on a hanger, have an electric plug attached to them, or you sleep on them, sit on them, walk on them, ride in them, or store things in them. Furniture, clothing, automobiles, home appliances, and electrical and electronic products are the major categories of consumer durables.

Critical to the success of new products here is new design, new technology, adding new features and new applications for existing technology, and providing new benefits, especially cost reductions based on improvements in the technology. In fashion goods, furniture, china, and tableware, design is often everything. New designs can be tested in focus groups and consumer panels to lessen the risk of the new product introduction. New technology and new applications of old technology are critical in such areas as consumer electronics and small electrical goods.

Sometimes the application of an already established technology to another product category can create a new market. For example, a major new product category, the food processor, is basically a new configuration of cutting blades, along with a strong industrial-level motor, attractively packaged and promoted to the gourmet cook. In other cases, an industrial product can be downsized and downpriced and marketed against a consumer market. Such was the case with home coffee brewing machines. These utilize the same coffee brewing technology as the large restaurant coffee urns. Mr. Coffee pioneered the introduction of this product to the consumer mass market, with a little help from Joe DiMaggio.

The critical success factors are somewhat different for the various categories of consumer durables.

## Consumer Electronics

More than any other category of consumer durables, consumer electronics is still technology driven. However, styling and design are becoming more important as technology brings these products closer and closer to the practical limits of perfection. As these products approach technical perfection, ironically they start assuming many of the characteristics of a fashion product. They are increasingly sold and differentiated primarily on the basis of styling and pricing rather than technical specs.

## Automobiles

Automobiles face perhaps the most complicated new product planning challenge of all! Here product planning is constrained by the Environmental Protection Agency (EPA), downsizing, fuel economy, environmental factors, increased segmentation and sophistication of the consumer market, and the need to simultaneously reduce costs and dramatically lessen defect and reject rates, among many other things. Most important, after years of believing that offering the consumer a bewildering array of options was the key to success, the Big Three are now devoting enormous efforts to convincing their dwindling customers that they do indeed have a quality level as good as Honda, Toyota, and Nissan.

Automotive product planning emphasis has shifted from

a marketing driven approach which offered a wide range of accessory options to a product planning driven approach that emphasizes quality of manufacture, reliable operation, safety, and low operating cost. Unfortunately, this major shift in product planning strategy came only after several multibillion dollar loss years at the Big Three auto companies in the early 1980s.

## Furniture/Furnishings

Niche marketing is widely practiced in this category. Life-style and demographic changes including second homes, condominiums, and smaller families have created specific new product planning opportunities. Products such as waterbeds appeal to specific life-style groups. Outdoor and patio furniture has grown apace with the rise of the barbecue culture in the Sunbelt states. However, some types of furniture associated with life-styles that are fading away, for example, formal dining rooms, parlors, and so on, are now struggling to maintain their sales volume.

## Fashion Merchandise

While fashions change quickly, this industry has been slow to adopt the product planning techniques, such as market research, utilized in other consumer goods categories. Speed of response time is still essential and here entrepreneurs still make multimillion dollar decisions on specific lines and styles based on "gut feelings.'

In fashion merchandising it is critical to be in tune with the dominant life-styles and values of the target market. In the late 1960s, the miniskirt conquered the fashion world because it expressed the spirit of youthful rebellion and embodied the freedom that was the hallmark of those turbulent years. When in the late 1980s designers tried to reintroduce the miniskirt, it was a total bomb, because the psychology and the mindset of the target market had completely changed.

# CHAPTER TWENTY-EIGHT

# New Products in Japanese Companies

Many American companies would be well advised to study in detail how their Japanese competitors, and Japanese companies in general, go about the process of bringing new products to market.

In my experience, Japanese companies, and especially those in high-tech and other industrial categories, spend more time, effort, and money on new products than do their American counterparts. Perhaps most important, new products are not the special responsibility of a small group of specialists working in relative isolation from the rest of the company, as is so often the case in American companies.

Indeed, new product planning is part of the warp and woof of every job in the Japanese company, from the *Keicho* (chairman) to the people on the assembly line. Japanese engineers and product designers take enormous pride in their work, and take special pains to ensure a successful product launch, often doing things that many hard-nosed American financial executives would never permit.

For example, a Japanese executive considers it a personal disgrace if a product for which he is responsible is found to be poorly made or to have some sort of operating defect. I have personally seen numerous instances where a Japanese firm flies teams of technicians and engineers to the United States to make field adjustments and perform additional quality control checks on products already shipped to retailers or customers.

The Japanese new product planning process is elaborate and painstaking, but it often moves more quickly than its American counterpart. Market research often is utilized more intensively and more consistently by Japanese companies than by their American competitors.

But contrary to U.S. popular opinion, the vast majority of Japanese products are first introduced to the Japanese domestic market. Only the fittest survive the fierce competition of this market and are then brought to the American market.

These survivors are the products that make their way to American shores, and therein lies their main challenge. Sometimes it is necessary to repackage, reposition, or reconfigure the product to meet specific needs of the American market. Japanese firms such as Sony, Matsushita, Nissan, Honda, and Toyota that have made serious efforts to become true multinational or global firms accomplish this transition better than those that have not. Japanese companies that have not yet admitted their American executives to the inner circle of market planning and product planning may lack critical inputs that can make a difference when the new product is introduced to the American market.

The Japanese, a people to whom nuance and subtlety are all-important, not surprisingly show a strong preference for pastel shades and delicate colors. American consumers, who find subtlety to be wimpish and nuance to be confusing, prefer strong, stark colors in their imported Japanese products. Failure to adapt the colors to the American market can seriously retard acceptance of the product in the American market.

Japanese companies also pay much attention to the packaging of these products for the American market. The product usage brochures, instructional materials, and similar communications materials are often prepared afresh by American expatriates resident in Japan, rather than using a stilted translation from the Japanese.

The more sophisticated Japanese companies are increasingly aware of the special nature of the American market. Therefore, they often custom-tailor their products for the American market, even if this cuts into their passion for long, uniform factory runs. Japanese product planners frequently visit the American market, meet with key customers, and make a sincere effort to understand the life-styles, preferences, needs, and demands of their American customers.

Further, Japanese firms with American subsidiaries make it a practice to send young engineers and marketing people to work in their American subsidiaries as "trainees," usually for a two- or three-year stint. These people will return to the Japanese parent company in responsible positions, equipped with a strong hands-on knowledge of the American market. Veteran American salespeople at these Japanese firms learned long ago to "always be nice to your Japanese trainee because some day this trainee will be your boss."

Most important, the Japanese new product planning process is not dominated by financial planning people with a short-run focus on next quarter's "bottom line." I have seen many Japanese companies go the extra mile and then some, to introduce major new breakthrough products. The Keicho in a Japanese firm who believes in a new product will accept losses in a new product introduction that American competitors are unwilling or unable to accept.

Japanese companies, especially those in high-tech industries, are also more willing to accept the validity of an extended "market makeready period" to introduce a breakthrough product or a major new technology than are their U.S. competitors.

New product planning and development is a respected and prestigious activity in the Japanese firm. It demands and receives the total effort and allegiance of talented people who are going to work out their careers in the company. The handful of American companies that have developed new product planning cultures similar to those of the rank and file of Japanese companies have been uniformly successful.

# CHAPTER TWENTY-NINE

# New Products in High-Technology Companies

New product planning entails a special set of problems and opportunities in high-technology companies. Forget the glamour side of high-technology products. Focus instead on the tough realities of most high-technology product planning and marketing:

• *The time window in which you will have a technology advantage over your competitors grows smaller every year.* Half of all the scientific inventions and technology advancements since the time of the Cro-Magnons have occurred in the 1980s.

The small, sharply focused high-technology companies in such areas as robotics, biotechnology, electronic components, and aerospace have a special need to focus on the activities of present and potential competitors. Technology forecasting and competitive analysis need to be integral components of their new product planning process.

• *It is very easy for competitors to copy, reverse-engineer, or just "rip off" most high-technology products.* In electronics, for example, the accelerated pace of technology makes the patent protection process almost useless as a defense against imitators. This is especially important when the imitator is a Far Eastern firm with high quality standards, a strong technology base, and a relatively low-paid, highly productive work force. Taiwan, South Korea, and Malaysia (and now even Thailand and India) are moving into this category.

• *Customers in high-technology industries are so jaded, so overwhelmed with innovative new products, that your breakthrough product, which required great technical or scientific feats to produce, is often greeted by the buyer with skepticism or indifference.* This is especially true if you neglect the publicity and marketing guidelines we have outlined for new products. Only a decade ago, the American consumer was amazed at a VCR recorder that provided one hour of recording and sold for $1,200. Today consumers take for granted the latest model VCR that records eight hours, can be programmed to go on and off automatically at preselected times, and can be purchased at the local electronics retailer for $239.

• *Perhaps most important, several high-technology industries, most notably consumer electronics, have a strong tradition of "cost down" or of major decreases in price of the product over the first few years of the product life cycle.* Because of this, many consumers are often reluctant to buy a new product in the first few years of its life cycle, preferring to wait for that big price drop that they know will come in a year or so. The more sophisticated consumer electronics companies are well aware of this consumer psychology and allow for it in their product introduction planning. The truly breakthrough product or the major new, improved, next-generation product is usually first marketed on a selective basis through high-end outlets, priced and promoted to appeal to "audiophiles, videophiles, or computer mavens," before it is sold to the mass market.

There is ample opportunity to have major new product introductions in high-technology industries that are both successful and financially profitable. Success in this instance requires very sharply focused market planning so that the new product is promoted and sold only to those market segments who are willing to pay up to be the innovator who owns that exciting new high-tech product.

# Mini-Histories

# 24

## Apple Computer

## The Importance of Strong Professional Advisors

The saga of Steve Jobs and Steve Wozniak toiling in a garage to design and produce the first Apple Computers has become part of the folklore of American business. Rather than retell the basic story, I will focus on one aspect of the Apple success story that played a critical role but has been overlooked by the legions of writers who have reported the Apple story.

There are three kinds of specialized outside expertise that are vitally important to any start-up firm that hopes to make it big: (1) your legal counsel; (2) your investment banker or financial advisor, and (3) your public relations, image, and media advisor. Critical to the rapid success of Apple was the foresight of the founders in bringing in top flight professionals in each of these key specialties early in the startup process.

Bill Fenwick, a brilliant litigator and business attorney, was recruited as a board member and his law firm retained to handle the legal affairs of Apple during those critical early years. Hambrecht and Quist, which went on to become the leading investment advisor and venture capital firm for scores of Silicon Valley startups, was responsible for supplying Apple with startup capital and for developing the capital necessary to finance its very rapid early growth. Regis McKenna and his public relations firm were brought on board to develop the image, the message, and the persona of Apple and to help communicate this message to both the business world and the general public. When business analysts speculate on how Apple was able to grow so fast so long without falling apart in the classic Silicon Valley manner, the combined talents of Fenwick, McKenna, and the Hambrecht and Quist team were key elements in this success story.

For having the foresight to think big and to persuade

these top talents to apply their skills to their newborn company, for these and many other reasons, the "two Steves," the
charismatic founders of Apple, were rewarded with a first-
class and continuing Big Winner in the Apple Computer.

## Key Lesson

When a start-up company is introducing a major breakthrough
product, it should prepare a contingency plan to deal with the
challenges of instant success and very rapid growth. This
includes getting all the right support systems in place internal-
ly and recruiting the best and brightest people you can find
outside the company to advise in their areas of expertise
during this high growth period.

## Postscript

The two Steves and many of their entrepreneurial soulmates
have, of course, long since departed Apple to be replaced by
Pepsi Generation–type managers. This in no way diminishes
the glory of their accomplishments or the value of the lessons
of this mini-history.

# 25

## Cuisinart Food Processor

### How to Turn Your Retirement Hobby into a $100 Million Business

Carl Sontheimer served for many years as a professor of physics at Massachusetts Institute of Technology. Mr. Sontheimer decided to take early retirement in the 1970s to devote more time to his hobbies of gourmet cooking and traveling. During a trip to a food fair in France, Sontheimer came across a unique new food processing machine manufactured by a small French company called Robot Coupe. Intrigued by this machine, Sontheimer followed up and negotiated the rights to serve as American distributor for this food processor.

This machine, for which the name Cuisinart was coined, was a true breakthrough product. The Cuisinart Food Processor had a more powerful motor and a greater range of capabilities than any kitchen appliance then available in the American market.

Sontheimer very wisely decided to limit his distribution and his sales during the early years and to establish Cuisinart as an upscale product for the sophisticated gourmet chef. Distribution was limited to prestige department stores and retail outlets specializing in gourmet food equipment. Advertising was limited but awareness of the product spread rapidly via word of mouth recommendations. The Cuisinart was *the* prestige gift product for several holiday seasons.

This low-profile approach to market development was very wise, since it served to keep competition out of the market for several years. Sunbeam and Proctor Silex, and even General Electric with its sophisticated competitive analysis and planning systems, lost two years or more in responding to the success of Cuisinart.

By that time Cuisinart had developed a full line of products and had the market position and financial strength to hold its own against its larger but slower and less innovative competitors. Thus did Carl Sontheimer, a late-blooming entrepreneur, turn his retirement hobby into a profitable $100 million company and create a whole new category of household appliance. Truly a Big Winner as we measure market introductions.

## Key Lesson

When a startup company planning to market a breakthrough product has a number of large, well-established competitors, sometimes a gradual, low-key product introduction is the best approach. Cuisinart gained a vital two-year edge on its larger competitors because it didn't come on as a major threat to their business at the start. By the time major competitors recognized that Cuisinart had created a new category in the home appliance market, Cuisinart already had established itself in the marketplace.

# 26

## Maxim Wide Mouth Toaster

### It Does Indeed Pay to Have a Big Mouth

For many years the toaster was an unchanging staple product in the American home. It was plain and functional. It made two pieces of regular toast and it was manufactured by General Electric, Westinghouse, and a few other large companies. In the 1970s, people started consuming in large quantities such products as muffins, rolls, pita bread, bagels, waffles, frozen pastries, and thick-sliced bread. Yet the toaster-making giants were slow to respond to the need and the challenge presented by this changing pattern of bread consumption.

The Maxim Company, a small entrepreneurial consumer appliance company located in Newark, New Jersey, took a leadership position in developing and marketing the wide mouth toaster. Its product was simple but elegantly designed—bone white with the small Maxim logo in red. One wide, long toasting slot accommodated the many sizes and shapes of bread products that were now being eaten by Americans.

Priced, packaged, and promoted to the upscale, gourmet food–oriented market, the wide mouth toaster soon became the key item in the Maxim product line. Maxim has used the strength and the attractiveness of this niche product to help establish the company's full line of espresso makers, ovens and accessories, woks, and coffee makers.

The Maxim Company has built outward from its basic technical strength in manufacturing electric heating units by using imaginative product planning to produce products such as the wide mouth toaster.

At least a Modest Winner as we measure new product introductions, the Maxim wide mouth toaster helped the company to secure its niche in the competitive world of high-end gourmet kitchen appliances.

## Key Lesson

This case further illustrates the point that a small entrepreneurial company, able to move quickly, can establish a new niche in an established market before the industry giants are aware of or able to act on the opportunity. The giants may eventually enter the market in force with power advertising and competitive pricing. But, if the market introduction has been properly planned and executed, the entrepreneur will have taken the high end of the market and can often hold on against competition from the giants at least in this high-profit sector.

# 27

# Boil-in-the-Bag Indian Foods Company

## You Can't Do It All By Yourself

Boil-in-the-bag frozen foods have been the high growth segment of the fiercely competitive frozen foods business for several years. A subcategory, ethnic frozen entrées including the Benihana brand of Japanese food and various brands of Chinese and Mexican frozen foods entrées, have been especially successful with yuppies and the affluent, young singles market.

Our client, Indian by birth but long a U.S. resident and a sophisticated financial executive, decided to form a company to prepare and market Indian frozen boil-in-the-bag dinners. A short line of three product offerings was developed. All three scored very well on the various product tests we conducted. The formulations contained only mild doses of curry and were positioned not to the small number of Indian food lovers, but to the general market of young upscale consumers.

Our company conducted the basic market research, worked with the entrepreneur to develop the business plan, and helped to create the advertising positioning and market entry strategy.

However, the client needed a basic amount of start-up capital in order to achieve the critical mass of distribution and customer acceptance necessary for success. Although very hard-working and intelligent, he was unable to raise the minimum amount of start-up capital necessary to give this fledgling business a reasonable chance for success. The option of offering a substantial equity position to a marketing/sales professional who could secure distribution and shelf space in major chains was not compatible with his style or with his goals for the company.

For two frustrating years, we watched our entrepreneur client try to "do it all himself" and to introduce his products without advertising support in the most competitive section of the supermarket, the frozen foods section, and in the most competitive market, the greater New York metropolitan area. Finally, exhausted by his labors, our friend withdrew his product line from general distribution and is now marketing it on a limited basis through several Indian restaurants.

At this point the boil-in-the-bag Indian food market introduction must be rated as a Loser. But our client believes, and we agree, that if the funding necessary for a professional product launch could be obtained, the product line would still be successful in the market.

## Key Lesson

Chapter Twenty-Three stresses that the startup entrepreneurs often need a partner or a strong backup person who brings complementary skills or expertise to compensate for their shortcomings or their lack of time or resources. In this case, a partner or a marketing person with knowledge of the market and contacts with key buyers was the missing ingredient for the Boil-in-the-Bag Indian Foods Company.

# 28

## New Coke/Classic Coke

## Crisis Management in a Large, Complex Company

The Coca-Cola Company is widely regarded as one of the best-managed companies in the Free World. They are consistently profitable, both in good times and bad. The company has a distinctive culture, esprit, and a first-class marketing operation.

So when the Coca-Cola Company is perceived as producing a major bomb, it becomes front page news. The replacement of the old Coca-Cola with New Coke was widely considered to be that rare bomb. In 1985, fearful of losing market share to Pepsi, Coca-Cola introduced New Coke as a replacement for the beloved Coke that for generations had been a part of the life-style of hundreds of millions of people around the world.

This new product introduction had been in the planning stage for some years. While still the dominant cola drink in terms of market share, Coke had slowly and steadily been losing share points to Pepsi in the critical youth market. Pepsi's constant theme of the new Pepsi Generation plus the slightly sweeter taste of Pepsi were thought to be the reasons for this share erosion.

The new Coke was painstakingly tested in blind taste tests and other forms of research over an extended period of time. New Coke was rated very well against Pepsi and the "Old Coke" in these blind taste tests, especially among the youth market segment.

However, one key element was strangely omitted from the research. This was the fact that the new Coke was to be a replacement for, as opposed to an addition to, the traditional Coca-Cola. Coke did not sufficiently consider the tremendous emotional attachment of millions of Americans to the old Coca-Cola. As one analyst noted, "More than any other single product, Coca-Cola *is* America."

After a great uproar from their bottlers and key customers, Coca-Cola bowed to demand and very quickly reinstated "Classic Coke." However, New Coke was tragically wounded by all this confusion and now limps along with a 2 to 3 percent market share. Surely a Loser as new product introductions are measured.

## Key Lesson

Coca-Cola, a large, complex multinational company with an elaborate planning system, proved that when confronted with a crisis, it was capable of making a major decision quickly and implementing it very professionally. The skillfully renamed Classic Coke was back on the retail shelves very quickly and the long-term damage was minimal. Many business writers have speculated that Coca-Cola masterminded this entire scenario. I believe Coke management. They made a rare goof, but the crisis management response they engineered is the envy of many large bureaucratic companies.

# 29

## IBM Electronic Selectric Composer

### A Winner Takes the Time to Do It Right

In the early 1970s, I had some trepidation when assigned to my first client study for IBM. The computer giant was thought of in Olympian terms but I relished the opportunity to study firsthand its unique approach to bringing new products to market.

The product was the electronic selectric composer, designed to be sold to composition houses and inhouse print shops. A small firm from Boston called Compugraphic had marketed such a device in the late 1960s and had made heavy inroads into the business IBM had traditionally enjoyed in that market segment.

The work involved in-depth interviews with many present and potential customers to provide input for product planning, pricing, market introduction, and reactions of the market to the Compugraphic product offering. Expecting a very dynamic, aggressive client, we were surprised by the thoroughness and excessive concern with small detail of the client personnel we worked with.

Subsequently, we found out our project team was only one of three that had been assigned to study this market independent of each other. Only if all three come back with a "go" recommendation would IBM move forward, according to our project coordinator. He was less concerned with speed than with developing a very thorough market introduction plan: "We may not be first, but once we have the right product and the right plan, we will have thirty-five hundred salespeople hitting every available prospect within several weeks," was his analysis.

IBM did indeed introduce the electronic selectric composer, and it was, as you might expect, a Big Winner. The product has gone through many upgrades and revisions over the years, but it was for many years a staple ingredient in the IBM product line.

## Key Lesson

When you are the largest and most powerful company in the business, it sometimes takes longer to plan and orchestrate your new product introduction. This sometimes permits your competitor to gain some time window of advantage. But if you hit the ground running with a total plan, you can often make up for the lost time. This technology product was not a breakthrough product, but it managed to become dominant because of the superior marketing and service capability of IBM.

# 30

## Continuous Casting Equipment

## But We Have Always Done It This Way

In the mid-1960s, the major American steel manufacturers were riding high: Demand for the various finished and semi-finished steel products was high, profits were steady and growing, and the world looked rosy indeed. Wages were far above those of Third World and Pacific Rim countries but imports were not yet a serious problem.

During the late 1960s, American DeMag, a subsidiary of DeMag of Duisburg, Germany, retained our services to investigate the market potential for a radically new approach to steel making. This new process, called continuous casting, involved considerable upfront cost for new equipment. However, the new process permitted the elimination of a number of intermediate product stages and allowed for considerable reduction in the cost of the final steel product.

We interviewed about twenty steel manufacturers in the course of this work. The engineers were quick to note that continuous casting indeed had cost advantages over the traditional method for producing certain categories of product, especially for short runs. However, each steel manufacturer elected to remain with the basic process that had been used for decades because "we have always done it this way."

The major Japanese, Korean, and other Far East steel makers did indeed pick up on the continuous casting process, and the rest is history. During the past decade the American steel industry has gone through crisis after crisis and has melted down to less than one-half of its mid-1960s size in terms of total employment and volume of production. United States Steel Corporation employment stood at 94,000 in 1974. USX, the successor of U.S. Steel, today has fewer than 30,000 employees. The United Steel Workers Union now has more people drawing pensions than employed in unionized steel mills.

One cannot say that the only reason for the troubles of American steel manufacturers is the failure to accept continuous casting equipment when it was first available and they had the profits to pay for it. But surely the mindset that we encountered in our study was both a symptom and a cause of their problems.

Thought to be a Loser by the tradition-bound old-line steel companies in the mid-1960s, Continuous Casting Equipment was a Big Winner with the aggressive and imaginative Far East competitors of the U.S. "Big Steel" oligopoly.

## Key Lesson

The Bible says "pride goeth before a fall." No major industry was more proud and more complacent than the American steel industry a generation ago. And no industry has fallen so far so fast as did the American steel industry in the 1980s. The rigid mindset of the American steel industry, set at the turn of the century when Andrew Carnegie created Big Steel, was unable to change in the 1960s to accommodate the new reality.

# 31

## Pioneer RT701/707 Tape Recorder

## The Last Hurrah for the Reel-to-Reel

When a new technology begins to overtake and supplant an old, established technology, conventional wisdom calls for concentrating product development and R&D effort on the new technology to the neglect of the old technology.

The reel-to-reel tape recorder, a large and expensive machine, had long been favored by audiophiles and music lovers. However, in the late 1970s, advances in the technology of cassette tape decks including longer playing time, auto reverse, lower prices, and enhanced sound quality led many consumers to choose cassette tape decks rather than reel-to-reel systems.

Cognizant of this trend, most of the established reel-to-reel manufacturers hastened to get into the cassette tape deck market and neglected to apply technology enhancements to their reel-to-reel products. Recognizing an opportunity, Pioneer Electronic Corporation invested considerable time, money and talent into a downsized, attractively priced, reel-to-reel tape recorder that had the auto reverse feature.

The product was immediately accepted by the audiophiles, who still considered reel-to-reel to be superior to cassette tape decks. During a two-year-plus life cycle, while the total reel-to-reel consumer market continued its slow decline, Pioneer increased its own market share from 9 to 27 percent in this product category.

This new, improved, next-generation product also enhanced the image of Pioneer among the serious audiophiles, enabling the company to increase its market penetration in that segment and to improve its overall distribution through retail outlets catering to the high end of the market.

By having the courage and imagination to swim against the tide, Pioneer was rewarded with a Big Winner with its downsized line of reel-to-reel tape recorders, the RT701/707.

## Key Lesson

This case illustrates some of the key differences between Japanese and American product planning philosophy. When a product category is on a long, slow, secular decline, the standard American wisdom is to milk it for profits (the "cash cow theory"), rather than investing in new, improved, next-generation products. Frequently this is a correct strategy but in many technology-driven industries, some creative R&D or product development applied to this mature product can give it a new life and permit huge increases in market share against your competitors who are busily milking their cash cows. The Japanese continue to apply new technology to their product introductions unencumbered by the latest new management theory.

## Winning Ideas

1. The start-up company faces the twin challenges of establishing a company while developing a new, often breakthrough product. The entrepreneur founder is usually well advised to concentrate his or her personal energy on the product, delegating administrative issues to competent associates.

2. The entrepreneurial company needs to establish at least a barebones new product planning process that provides some feedback from the marketplace and from the close associates of the founder.

3. Large, complex companies need to keep the new product planning process lean, mean, and professional. Key product planning team members should be people who are "into the product," while professional staff support people contribute in their areas of expertise.

4. For consumer packaged goods products, equal time and attention in the new product planning process must be given to the "three Ps"—the product itself, the packaging, and the positioning of the product against the target market and competition.

5. Product planning for consumer durables must focus on technology, life-style issues, and fashion or design issues depending on the nature of the product.

6. Most large Japanese companies have sophisticated and well-developed new product planning processes. Japanese companies place great faith in market research and usually do a careful analysis of the American market before introducing a product even if it has already been successful in Japan. They also provide young Japanese executives with practical "hands-on" experience in the American market, early in their career.

7. High-technology companies must prepare for patent infringement, reverse engineering, and knock-off products, as well as the tendency of customers to resist purchasing the new product when first introduced, in the expectation that there will be substantial cost-down within the next several years.

# SECTION V

# PRESERVING THE COMPETITIVE EDGE

In this last section I treat several key issues that, if properly handled, will help your company preserve the competitive advantage that should come with a successful new product introduction. These issues are as follows:

- Preparing, as part of your market entry strategy, a series of responses to meet the competition that will follow a successful new product launch
- Securing a patent, which often guarantees two or three years of solid profits
- Developing a very tight set of policies and procedures on new product confidentiality, which will also help preserve your winning edge.
- A most effective way to build on success is to start immediately to develop a new, improved, next-generation product.

In addition, I offer some practical suggestions for speeding up the process of bringing new products to market and communicating the results of your new product activity to the all-important financial community.

# CHAPTER THIRTY

# Meeting the Competition

The first law of physics is that every action brings an opposite and equal reaction. This law also applies to new product introductions.

The time to start planning to meet the competition is before, not after, you introduce your new product.

Some or all of your competitors are going to do one or more (or possibly all) of the following once your new product starts to make an impact:

- Cut the price of their own directly competing product in order to hold onto market share.
- Increase their own advertising or sales promotion effort or dealer incentives on behalf of their own competing product.
- Use various "dirty tricks" to cast doubt on the value or reliability of your new product.
- For a technical breakthrough product or a new, improved, next-generation product, you can expect that they will immediately "reverse engineer" the product and determine what it will cost them to produce the product themselves at various levels of sales volume.

A thorough new product planning process considers these possible reactions long before the fact and factors the results of these competitive reactions into the sales forecast and market introduction plan long before competitors have a chance to impact your plans. Again, the doctrine of "no surprises" is key to success.

An analysis of the past history of competitors will usually give you a good indication as to their potential reaction. World-class competitors usually fight hard, but they fight clean. They are more likely to move quickly to remedy the breach in their own product line that your new product has created. Less well-run competitors or those who lack the resources or the vision to compete with you on new products will be more likely to resort to price cutting and/or disparagement.

The product planning and marketing people, working together, should commit to paper their best combined analysis of the likely reaction of each major competitor to your new product under two sets of conditions, modest success for the new product, and big success for the new product.

The following are some of the many ways in which you might meet these competitive reactions.

• *Cut price.* If you anticipate a competitive reaction based on price, your initial pricing strategy should provide adequate room for you to maneuver in terms of straight price reductions, volume rebates, or other approaches to beating the price competitors at their own game.

• *Increase advertising and promotion.* When the competitor increases advertising and promotion effort on behalf of its own product, your own advertising and promotion should also increase. More important, it should focus on the superior features and benefits offered by your new product as opposed to your competitor's old product.

• *Make use of disparagement or dirty tricks.* If your competitor chooses this approach to your new product, be prepared to play hardball. Scrutinize the competitor's ads for false or misleading claims, be quick to rebut false claims made to your dealers, call a national dealer or sales rep meeting if necessary, and flood your trade media with press releases and facts to get the true story out.

• *Develop a me-too version of your product.* Even if the competitor's me-too product has new performance features, you still have the psychological and the tactical advantage. By now you should have the prime retail shelf space, the consumer brand awareness, and the buyer loyalty. Your competitor must try, at great cost, to win these away from you. Determine your competitor's pain threshold and corporate profit picture and estimate if and to what extent your raising the stakes of the game will cause the competing firm to back off from attacking you in order to preserve its corporate profits.

Figure 30-1 summarizes the range of competitors' likely reactions to your successful new product.

**Figure 30-1.** Likely reactions of competitors to your successful new product.

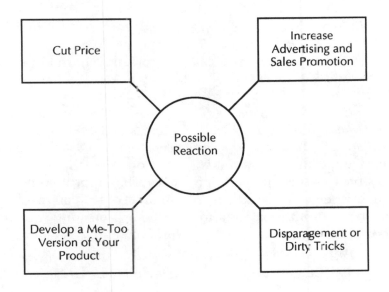

# CHAPTER THIRTY-ONE

# New Products and Patent Protection

Patent law is a special area of expertise, and I make no claims to expert standing in this area. However, as a business planner I have been involved in a number of new product introductions where patents have been granted and others where patent protection was not sought or the patent was improperly drawn.

When you have patent protection, you have options not available in other situations. You can prepare a more aggressive marketing plan or you can plan on supernormal profits.

Several basic rules need to be stated.

1. *If there is anything about the new product that has even a remote chance of receiving patent protection, by all means go for it! The potential cost is small compared with the potential value of the patent.* Your patent attorney will advise you on whether "prior art" exists on your idea or not. Sometimes what appear to be very mundane new technical ideas can indeed be patentable. A consultation with a patent attorney about protecting your new product will almost always be a worthwhile investment.

2. *Patents are especially helpful when the company is small or startup.* Patents are a great way of gaining instant credibility

with customers, trade press, salespeople, and, most important, Wall Street and the investment community.

The fact that a product or a key feature of the product is patented will encourage reps to carry your line, retailers to stock your product, and end customers to try it. Most people equate patent protection with easy sales and high profit margins, so don't overlook these marketing and distribution side benefits of patent protection.

3. *The Patent Office is one of those rare branches of the federal government that is highly professional and has its act together.* If your discovery is truly unique you will get your patent in a great majority of cases. If you are turned down, specific reasons for rejection are provided. You have the options of recasting and resubmitting the patent, appealing the Patent Office decision, or going to market without the patent.

In any event, the very act of filing the patent, for which the fee is indeed modest, will clarify the status of your product relative to patent protection.

4. *Establish a "war chest" of money to be used to litigate with people who try to "rip off" or infringe your patent.* If the patent is granted and the product is successful in the marketplace, it follows as surely as night follows day that someone will introduce a competing product.

Set up a network of people, including salespeople, reps, customers, your own employees, and friends in the trade media to keep a close watch for any present or potential patent infringement. And have a set of standing instructions with your attorney to move quickly with injunctions and other legal remedies against people who infringe your patent.

5. *Apply for patent protection not only for the way your product works but for every theoretically possible way that the product can be made to work.* This is called "building a bridge" around the technology and is often very helpful in keeping competitors from legally devising another approach to providing the unique benefit that your product provides.

There are often several ways that the product can be configured or designed to yield the unique benefit that is derived from your potential product. If in the process of developing your patent you discovered these alternate technologies, these should also be patented, whenever possible.

6. *In your business planning, assume a maximum of two to three years of "supernormal profits" from your patent protected products.* Almost certainly, some competitor will find a way, legal or illegal, to neutralize or negate some or all of the effect of your patent within that time. Foreign competitors, especially those in several small Far East countries, are not put off by patent protection. They will find a way to market a product that does all or most of what your patented product does, often for a fraction of the cost.

So get the best patent advice available, do it quickly, and do it professionally. The patent is typically good for seventeen years. But don't plan on more than two or three years to skim the cream of the market before competition forces your profits back down into the normal range of profits for the product and the industry.

All too often inventors, especially first-time entrepreneur-inventors, assume that their patent will protect them against competition for the full life of the patent. This is a naive and dangerous assumption. Figure that at best you will have two or three years of supernormal profits. After that, you will have to fight hard for every profit dollar.

# CHAPTER THIRTY-TWO

# New Products and Confidentiality

Nearly every company that introduces new products on a more or less regular basis has, or should have, a set of established procedures designed to keep information about new products away from competitors.

Indeed, a whole subset of the management consulting industry has grown up to provide competitive intelligence on new product activities for their clients.

Here are some recommendations regarding confidentiality:

1. *Draft a strong statement of policy regarding new product confidentiality and review it with your attorney.* After this legal review, require all key employees, manager level and above, to sign it. Also, executive secretaries, mailroom employees, people who work the copiers and fax machines, and anyone else who is in a position to see any confidential papers related to the new product also should be required to sign the confidentiality agreement. In addition, you should require all technical product development people to sign an additional document that grants complete rights in any technology, process, or product that they invent to the company.

2. *Mark each page of every paper that deals with new products with this confidentiality statement.* This confidentiality statement

should also note that making extra copies of the confidential material is not permitted.

3. *Number all copies of confidential papers and deliver them only to a specific authorized person.* Needless to say, none of these confidential materials should be removed from company offices without permission.

4. *Don't hire job hoppers, especially in key product planning positions or sensitive marketing positions.* Most important, you want to do everything in your power to prevent the situation whereby people build and develop new products at your expense in your R&D facility only to leave the company and set up in business in direct competition to you.

5. *Put each key person who works closely with new products under contract.* This includes sales managers, product managers, market researchers, as well as R&D people. On the one hand, the security of having a contract has value for them. The quid pro quo is that the contract prohibits them from working for a competitor or starting a directly competing business for a reasonable period of time after the end of the contract.

# CHAPTER THIRTY-THREE

# Planning for the Follow-Up Product

For the past year or more, you and your company have been running full out, straining every muscle to build the customer base and conduct normal business by day, while you have been devoting evenings, weekends, and any other time you can steal to the task of developing, testing, and planning the introduction of that major new product.

You have just finished producing the first samples, holding the press conference, and getting the sales representatives and salespeople all charged up to write orders on the new product.

It is now time to take a deserved rest and savor your accomplishments while the orders pour in. Right? Wrong! Chapter Thirty makes the point that if your new product is a winner, your competitors will immediately begin to reverse engineer the product to figure out how to knock it off or, more likely, how to bring out their own new, improved version at a lower cost—often within six to nine months.

So the time window of exclusivity is often going to be short on your new product introduction.

This means, if you are to hold and build on the strategic advantage created by your new product, you and your product planning team must *immediately* begin work on your own version of the new, improved, second-generation model at a lower price, if you have not already done so.

Sophisticated new product planners instinctively think in terms of two, three, or more generations of the new product, with appropriate time frames, at the time they are first fleshing out the new product concept.

In such cases, development work on the second-generation product is well under way before the first product hits the market.

Because you were the innovator who brought this new product (usually a breakthrough product) to market, you will have a decided competitive edge when you bring out your own new, improved, next-generation product. Your new, improved, second-generation product may not be especially superior to the product your competitor has rushed to the market. But since you have the image in the marketplace of being the innovator, you have a decided psychological edge on competition when you bring out your own new, improved, next-generation product.

You need another new product effort. But you won't get there by resting on your laurels. The standard line of Bernie Simmons, my first sales manager, is also very appropriate to the issue of developing the follow-up or new, improved, next-generation product. Bernie would greet us every morning by saying, "I love you baby, but what have you done for me lately?"

# CHAPTER THIRTY-FOUR

# Speeding Up the Process of Bringing New Products to Market

New products almost always seem to take longer to create and cost more money to bring to the market than had been budgeted or scheduled.

Often, there are time/money tradeoffs in the new product development process. By putting more people, resources, and money against the project, it is often possible to substantially reduce the new product development time frame.

Research from the consulting firm of McKinsey & Company, as reported by *Fortune* magazine, *How Managers Can Succeed by Speed;* February 13, 1989, strongly supports (for high-tech products at least) the strategy of throwing more people, money, and resources at the new product to meet the target date rather than controlling the budget and letting the launch date slip by six months or more. High-tech products introduced six months late, but on budget, forfeit one-third of their long-term profit. Products introduced on time but 50 percent over budget surrender only 4 percent of their projected profit, according to McKinsey and *Fortune*.

There are also trade-offs of some degree of management approval and control to permit more delegation of authority to the people who are actually designing the product. In many cases, the need for clearing major decisions with top management slows down the entire process.

I will now summarize a few simple concrete steps that companies, large and small, can take that will drastically reduce the time frame from the generation of a new product concept to the time of market introduction:

1. *Thoroughly review all steps in your process of bringing new products to market, with an eye to removing all unnecessary steps.* Some large, bureaucratic companies have developed overly complicated, cumbersome approaches to the act of generating, creating, and marketing new products. They become obsessed with micromanagement, and especially with the expense control side of new projects. It is often a wise decision to sacrifice some degree of cost control to meet the time demands of the market.

2. *Shift the focus of control from management and finance to creative entrepreneurship by the product planners.* Often, in large bureaucratic companies, decisions to spend even modest amounts of money must go through a cumbersome, time-consuming approval and authorization process. *A Passion for Excellence* by Tom Peters and Nancy Austin (Random House, 1985) describes how various product champions had to scrounge needed parts for important projects and how they had to ingeniously evade the stifling restrictions placed on the creative act of developing new products by the bean counters. Inspiring reading, but as my Uncle Morris said years ago, "Is this any way to run a business?"—especially in the fiercely competitive entrepreneurial world of the 1990s.

3. *Conduct various key activities in parallel rather than in a sequential process.* This approach has been tried with success in many high-tech companies. Market research, prototype development, systems engineering, manufacturing planning, and market introduction planning need not be separate sequential activities. They often can and should be conducted simultaneously.

This is perhaps the most impactful change that your company can implement to speed up the new product development process. Entrepreneurs, who often have the gifts of being able to see around corners and parallel processing, often instinctively work in this mode. This is yet another reason why entrepreneur-led firms so often outperform the large companies which are weighted down by their control-oriented systems.

4. *Support the people performing the product planning or R&D activity, and delegate more decision-making authority to them, while still monitoring progress on a regular basis.* In addition to greater control over financial decisions, the product planning people should be permitted to make all decisions necessary to keep the project moving along on or close to schedule, again with full and frequent reporting to management.

5. *Begin work early on the manufacturing process or the service delivery capability necessary to produce the new product.* One of the secrets of the success of German and Japanese companies in marketing new products is that they devote significantly more resources to developing new products than do their American competitors.

*Fortune* magazine's May 5, 1991, issue on manufacturing ("U.S. Manufacturing Is Back, pp. 55–56) notes that American companies put two-thirds of their resources into developing the new product and only one-third into creating the manufacturing process needed to produce the product. Japanese and Germans firms reverse these ratios. Moreover, the Japanese get a fast start on new products by simultaneously designing the new product and the manufacturing process needed to make it.

6. *A three-level budget for time and money for product planning and R&D should be prepared before the project is started.* While the middle-case forecast is usually the official budget, management must accept the possibility of the conservative or worst-case budget for bringing new products to market. If management is not prepared to live with this worst-case budget, they are not really committed to the new product and probably should not undertake the project at all.

Shifting to the conservative case often means either spending more money, adding more people, letting the launch date slip, or some combination of the three. But sometimes these decisions are necessary to get that winning new product, so vital to the success of the company, out into the marketplace.

Figure 34-1 summarizes the key strategies required to speed up the process of bringing new products to market.

**Figure 34-1.** How to speed up the process of bringing new products to market.

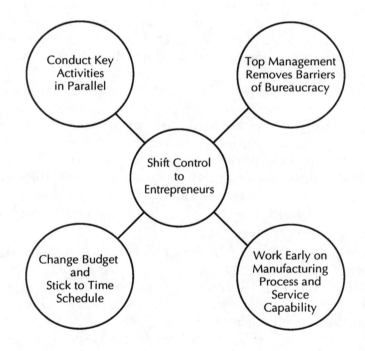

# CHAPTER THIRTY-FIVE

# New Products and Wall Street

The term *Wall Street* is a shorthand that covers market makers, stock brokers, investment bankers, venture capitalists, financial analysts, and mergers and acquisitions specialists. In other words, the people who determine the price of your stock and the value of your company, should you choose to sell it. In the case of the small entrepreneur, this may be your local banker or perhaps some silent partners, but the principles are valid in any case.

Certainly in the long term, and usually in the short term, some of these Wall Street people determine the ultimate payout that you and your company will receive from your efforts in bringing new products to market and in building a profitable business.

If your company is listed on one of the stock exchanges or is traded over the counter on NASDAQ, it is critical that the specialist or market makers who handle your stock be given continuing updates on the status of your new product development programs and the prognosis for the new products you are currently developing.

All too many companies, in our experience, ignore or give short shrift to this all important aspect of their marketing communications program. And those who do think to include the market makers, specialists, and financial analysts who cover the company in their communications tend to use the "big bang" rather than the "steady state" approach to communication with Wall Street.

They invite these key financial people to the once-a-year press party or to the gala new product introduction. But they ignore the need to provide the steady state stream of information on new products that builds confidence, and permits these financial people to make informed judgments and to recommend the stock with true conviction.

The critical issue and the critical word here is *confidence*. In short, the suppliers of capital and the market makers for the stock must have confidence that your new products are going to make it to market, are going to be accepted by your customers, and are going to make money for the company. And this confidence building is best accomplished by a program of full and continuing communication and honest dialogue, not by glitzy one-time, prepackaged shows.

You should develop a written company policy on marketing communications to the financial community relative to new products. This policy should be drafted by the chief financial officer or the president and should be subjected to close review by your legal counsel. Implementation of this policy relative to financial public relations should be carried out by your marketing communications people and your product development and marketing management.

A key element in this policy should be to schedule periodic "show and tell" sessions at the factory or the product development laboratory or wherever important new products are being readied for market introduction. The people who participate in these analyst–market maker briefings or "show and tell" meetings need to be carefully briefed beforehand on the level and type of additional information that may be provided.

It is essential to thoroughly rehearse for these meetings ahead of time. The questions that are likely to be asked, the replies to be given, and the people designated to answer them should be rehearsed and preplanned. It is especially important that this "steady state" of information on new products deal with the problems, frustrations, and delays along with the positive news.

The point of this preplanning is not to restrict the flow of information to which the financial community is entitled, but rather to ensure that facts and analyses are clearly separated from conjectures and forecasts relative to the new product. It is especially important that junior people not be permitted either to give vent to their frustrations or to give unduly rosy predictions about the prospects for a new product.

Most important, small and start-up companies should avoid like the plague the type of "boiler room" market maker who is interested in running up the price of your stock to unrealistic and unsustainable highs, mainly for his or her own benefit. You should check very carefully the credentials and track record of any potential market maker or broker dealer. Long-term membership in the New York Stock Exchange, the American Stock Exchange, or both is usually a good indication that the broker dealer is a solidly established firm that will follow ethical practices in the course of their market making activities.

A relatively small number of companies that frequently bring new products to market have developed considerable skill in this type of communication with the financial community. Most of them have been amply rewarded for their efforts in terms of enhanced stock prices and improved price earnings ratios over companies that neglect this form of marketing communication or that do it badly or only sporadically.

# Mini-Histories

# 32

## Compact Audio Disc Players

### Getting It All Together to Eliminate Confusion

Every so often, there comes along a breakthrough product of truly revolutionary proportions. Such a product is the compact audio disc player and the discs that play on it.

This product has achieved great success in the market with sales of over 8 million players and 25 million plus discs in the first four years since market introduction. The compact audio disc technology, which is similar in many respects to the videodisc technology, was developed over a number of years by Philips and Sony working at first alone and later in cooperation.

Both Sony and Philips had learned over many years of introducing new products that a revolutionary breakthrough product was, in itself, no guarantee of success in the marketplace. Over the preceding decades a number of breakthrough products, including the videodisc player and the VCR, had been introduced to the market in two or more incompatible formats. This caused confusion among consumers and required dealers to carry duplicate inventories thus reducing the profit potential of the breakthrough product.

The process by which musical sound is digitized and cleaned to provide the astonishing clarity and beauty of the compact disc recording is a complicated one that admits of many variations.

Some competitors were busily at work developing incompatible formats utilizing the same basic technology. Sony and Philips recognized that it was in everyone's interest to speed up the establishment of one standard compact disc format in the marketplace.

If the usual "format war" had been permitted to occur, two or three years of valuable market introduction time would have been lost, as consumers stood by while the format issue was being resolved in the marketplace.

Therefore, they worked to develop consensus for their format, by sharing experience and technology with competitors. By taking a farsighted and statesmanlike approach to introducing the compact audio disc player, Sony and Philips dramatically reduced the time it would take for the compact disc player to become a Big Winner in the American market.

## Key Lesson

Bernie Mitchell, one of the early marketing greats of the consumer electronics business, often closed his sales meetings by saying, "Confusion is the enemy." There is no question that for a number of consumer electronics products the net effect of the introduction of competing incompatible formats, Beta versus VHS in videocassette recorders, laser versus capacitance in videodiscs, was to confuse the consumer and, most important, to motivate him or her to defer purchase until the format war was decided. This trap was avoided in the introduction of the compact disc, and the result was near-instant success.

# 33

## Stereo Rack Systems

# Changing Your Philosophy to Meet Changing Markets

The hi-fi audio business started among the audio purists, who had a strong preference for building their own stereo system choosing the best units from each manufacturer. Thus, an audiophile would mix and match a receiver, turntable, tape deck, and speakers from three or four different manufacturers to build a dream system.

Our analysis of the hi-fi audio market in the mid-1970s showed a household penetration rate of 31 percent with customers whose average age was 24 years and who were almost exclusively male. After several years of the industry trying to broaden the market to include older, upscale, and married customers, our research indicated that these customers were put off by the complexity of the purchase decision. They preferred a one-decision, one-manufacturer system which came in an attractive stereo rack. They wanted to buy appearance, simplicity, and reliability, along with that great stereo sound.

To the old-time audiophile purists in the Pioneer organization, the concept of selling package systems to less than sophisticated customers went against their entire philosophy. However, it was recognized that for the product category to grow to its full potential in the market, ways had to be found to package and merchandise stereo systems to this affluent but unsophisticated older market.

To develop this market, three things were necessary:

1. The styling of a series of very attractive stereo systems at four or more price points.
2. The development of a new advertising program which

completely repositioned stereo components against this new target market.

3. A new channel of distribution policy, since research indicated that older, square customers were not comfortable buying in hi-fi stores and in dealing with the young, hip salespeople who are employed by these stores. The department store became the chosen channel of distribution to implement this repositioning of the product.

With their typical patience and persistence, the Japanese executives of the parent company gradually brought their American subsidiary to accept this major change of philosophy and direction. Pioneer was rewarded in the late 1970s with at least a Modest Winner in their attempts to broaden the hi-fi market to older customers through the marketing of stereo rack systems.

## Key Lesson

To fully exploit the potential market for hi-fi stereo products, it was necessary to market the follow-up product, which packaged the various elements of the stereo system together with a cabinet, and sell them as a ready-made system to the mass or less sophisticated market.

# 34

## The *Baseball Encyclopedia*

### The Ultimate Statistics Book Keeps Getting Better

For baseball fans the game has always had two major attractions. The first is the game itself, which has entertained countless millions of people of all ages for over a century.

The second great attraction of baseball is the statistics of the game, the teams, and the players. Recognizing this reality, in the late 1960s Macmillan Publishing Company and Information Concepts Incorporated began a project to build a complete comprehensive database on major league baseball from the inception of the National League in 1876, through the 1968 season. The cooperation of major league baseball and the Baseball Hall of Fame in Cooperstown, New York, was secured. Lifetime statistics on every player who ever played from 1876 onward were assembled and compiled from various sources.

An editorial task force of six people, each with a different expertise but all baseball lovers, was assembled. A team of over twenty-five researchers and research supervisors was employed to compile, edit, and design the first *Baseball Encyclopedia,* which was published in 1969.

Conceived as a one-time venture, this breakthrough product was widely acclaimed by fans and specialists. I received a copy of the *Baseball Encyclopedia* as a bachelor party present. Through the years my interest in baseball waned but recently, prompted by a young son very interested in baseball statistics, it has waxed again.

For a year, we scoured bookstores looking for an update of the original *Baseball Encyclopedia,* but to no avail. Then we learned that the seventh edition had just been published and we hastened to acquire it. The modest success of the first edition persuaded Macmillan to issue new, updated editions every third year.

The seventh edition, which weighs in at 2,800 pages (up 500 pages from the first edition), also contains a number of new sections such as lists of all major trades. Sales of 40,000 to 50,000 units at a list price of $45 are conservatively predicted for the seventh edition.

By daring to think in truly encyclopedia terms, the editors at Macmillan and the hundreds of mostly unpaid collaborators have generated a continuing venture that is a source of profit, enjoyment, and pleasure to thousands of baseball fans. At least a Modest Winner by our standards, we salute all concerned with bringing to market the *Baseball Encyclopedia*.

## Key Lesson

A new book is indeed a new product, especially one that establishes a new genre a sports encyclopedia. Because each new edition provides updates of the career statistics of all active players, it is by definition a new, improved, next-generation product. But the *Baseball Encyclopedia* went further. Each edition added one or more new sections of information or new refinements of existing information that was not available in previous editions. Its success has also prompted the publication of encyclopedias for basketball and other major sports.

# 35

## The Cookster

### A Simple, Patented Approach to Food Preparation

One tends to think of patent protection as most relevant to high-technology products. But the ability to secure patent protection can often be critical to the success of even a basic kitchen appliance.

The Cookster is a simple product, a round metal cylinder with a series of wires and plastic clips attached. It fits snugly into a four- or five-quart saucepan. A nylon bag is attached to the plastic clips which permits boil-in-the-bag cooking of your own favorite recipes.

This new cooking method permits greater retention of vitamins and trace minerals, and also creates superior flavor. Cleanup is minimal since the cooking bag is merely thrown away, eliminating pot washing completely.

Our client, who spent seventeen years perfecting the Cookster, is a successful entrepreneur in an unrelated business. In the fiercely competitive world of kitchen appliances, his opportunity to reap the proper rewards of his labors would be minimal were it not for his foresight in securing patent protection for various features of his new approach to cooking.

We have conducted a series of focus groups and product taste tests on this new cooking method throughout the country. The research has been very encouraging among certain segments of the population. But this is a razor/razor blade product and long-term success will be measured by continued usage of the Cookster and continued purchase of replacement nylon bags, rather than by high-volume sales of the Cookster units. Thus, the Cookster would be very vulnerable to competition by the industry giants were it not for its strong patent protection.

## Key Lesson

Small companies and products that can easily be imitated are especially in need of patent protection whenever possible. The Cookster is just entering test market and it is too early to categorize its level of success. But a slow-build, low-key market introduction and strong patent protection will be critical to its long-term prospects.

# 36

## Jiffy Lube

## The J Team Didn't Follow the Right Game Plan

The disappearance of thousands of local neighborhood gas stations and the inability or reluctance of many of those that remain to provide fast, reliable basic auto maintenance services provided a unique window for Jiffy Lube.

The J Team concept was articulated and developed by founder James Hindeman, a charismatic former football coach. The J Team concept, as presented by Dick Van Patten in a series of radio, TV, and print ads, calls for a complete oil change, lube job, tire check, and checking/topping off of all other lubricants in a fast twelve minutes.

Hindeman decided to build Jiffy Lube International as a franchise operation. The company quickly established a leadership position in the emerging quick-lube segment of the auto aftermarket service business. Many industry analysts, impressed with the rapid growth of Jiffy Lube and the dynamic style of Hindeman, saw Jiffy Lube as the McDonald's of the auto aftermarket. Indeed, in our own work of conducting seminars on the car care mall phenomenon, Jiffy Lube was the "hot retailer" whose presence would entice many real estate developers to attend in the hope of "doing deals" with Jiffy Lube.

There are two game plans or strategies to follow in building a franchise operation. The McDonald's approach emphasizes quality control, selection of qualified owner/operators, and continual training of the franchisee and his or her people. Rapid growth comes later, once the infrastructure is firmly in place to support growth and a solid reputation for quality is established.

The second approach to franchise building looks more to Wall Street and the price of the stock than to slowly building a firm foundation for growth. In this scenario, franchises are sold wholesale to resellers, and rapid growth to reach the critical mass necessary to support a massive advertising program is given priority over training and close quality control over the franchisees.

Jiffy Lube has announced a quarterly loss of $35 million, a major writedown of assets, and the need to raise more capital or to sell the company. Indeed, at the time of writing, the company has been sold to Pennzoil, its oil supplier, and Hindeman has been replaced as chairman. It now appears Jiffy Lube followed the Wall Street–oriented scenario more than the tried and true McDonald's formula for building a winning franchise operation. So the Jiffy Lube breakthrough product, which had all the earmarks of a Big Winner until recently, is now starting to look a little bit like a Loser to Wall Street and to the world.

## Key Lesson

The basic rules for success in franchising are well developed and time tested. A franchise concept that is viable is essential and Jiffy Lube has that. But the discipline to follow the McDonald's formula was apparently lacking. Preoccupation with meeting the super-growth projections of Wall Street analysts led to some bad business decisions that temporarily derailed this high-performing company.

## Winning Ideas

1. A successful new product inevitably brings a response from your competition. This competitive response can be in the form of price cutting, advertising, me-too products, or dirty tricks. Be prepared in advance to deal with each of these approaches with countermeasures of your own.
2. You should seek a patent for every new feature, technology application, or unique product configuration that might qualify for a patent protection. You should patent protect not only the actual product design but also every other possible way the new innovation can be configured.
3. A strong policy relative to the confidentiality of new products needs to be established, implemented, and clearly monitored, no matter the size of your company.
4. Even before a major new product hits the market you should begin work on the new, improved, second-generation version of this product.
5. There are a number of specific strategies or techniques that you can employ that can dramatically reduce the time required to take a new product from the concept stage to the point of market introduction.
6. Conducting a number of the critical new product development activities in parallel rather than in a sequential mode is key to speeding up the new product development process.
7. The skill, consistency, and candor with which you communicate your new product story to the financial community will be a key factor in how they price your stock and how they value your company. The critical issue is credibility. This is best achieved by a steady-state program of press releases, personal visits to key analysts, and "show and tell" sessions demonstrating your product to the financial community.

# EPILOGUE

# Twelve Keys to Success in Bringing New Products to Market

This book has identified many critical success factors in bringing new products to market.

Here is a summary and discussion of the twelve most critical success factors that a company must cultivate to be a consistent winner with new product introductions.

1. *A sharp focus on customers' unsatisfied needs.* Ultimately each new product succeeds or fails based on its degree of acceptance or rejection by the customer. Power marketing, super salesmanship, and brilliant advertising can all help to maximize the potential of the new product. But if the new product fails to provide a value, feature, or benefit that your customers value at a price that appears reasonable relative to alternate products, your new product is going to fail. All new product planning should start from this fundamental proposition.

2. *Supportive corporate culture.* A corporate culture that supports, encourages, and rewards the development and marketing of a steady stream of innovative new products is perhaps the most important key to success. If you don't have one

in your company, then the establishment of such a culture is your top priority.

Changing a corporate culture is a long, slow, painful process. While the change must come from the top, it cannot be achieved by executive fiat. When the corporate culture is supportive of new product planning, product planners are given latitude to try new things and to take reasonable risks. When people's jobs are on the line over a new product, the failure rate grows. In all too many companies, the new product people are told in many ways, direct and indirect, "If this product bombs, you are dead, baby." This is hardly the atmosphere to encourage creativity and the healthy risk taking needed to successfully introduce a major new product.

It is not necessary or even practical to attempt to duplicate the full extent and range of incentives available to entrepreneurs within the relatively safe haven of the large corporation. However, in large, complex companies, it is possible and helpful to develop new incentives and reward systems that will motivate product planning people to work the superhuman hours often necessary to meet the product launch date.

3. *A teamwork approach to new products.* This means a realization that bringing new products to market successfully is everybody's job. A willingness on part of all departments to lend their talent and expertise to this process whenever called on is essential. While the core new products team should be kept lean, mean, and very professional, everyone in the organization should respond with speed, eagerness, and willingness to lend time, resources, and expertise when asked to help by the new product planning team.

4. *A new product planning process appropriate for the task.* The new product planning process often need not be highly sophisticated but it must be reasonable, logical, and capable of adapting itself to the specific needs of different types of products and different market situations.

Most important, the new product planning process needs to be thoroughly understood and accepted by all who participate in it. The process must also be flexible enough to bend to accommodate the particular needs of important products, especially breakthrough products.

5. *Professionalism in product planning and development.* The people who have responsibility in this area should be senior, well paid, and have stature and security. Product planning is not a dead-end job or a place to gracefully outplace burned-out salespeople or sales managers. Nor is it a place for inexperienced people to be sent to learn the business. Unfortunately, most companies consider the product planning function to be a staff rather than a line operation. And staff functions invariably have lower prestige and are considered less vital by top management than are line operations.

6. *Consistent funding support in good times and lean times.* The management team that resists the temptation to cut back on R&D and on new product development when profits fade will maintain a high-morale, high-quality product planning effort that will pay off over time. But just one product planning or R&D staff or funding cutback in response to bad earnings will kill off this high morale commitment to new products for years to come.

7. *Strong commitment to quality market research.* This means establishing a market research budget for new products up front rather than forcing new product people to play politics and plead for the funds necessary to conduct research in the marketplace.

This also means doing the thorough, in-depth research that provides high-quality results rather than a "quick and dirty" survey. It also means a willingness to commit yourself to the amount and type of research necessary to collect the facts and to properly analyze them so that new product decisions are really made based on specific feedback from the market rather than on the gut feel of the product planners.

8. *Build new products into your business plans.* The role of new products in the strategic business plan is spelled out in detail along with the procedures for generating them. A section in the business plan should be devoted to new products. This chapter will include a subsection on the expected role of new products in improving the sales, profits, and competitive position of the company during the duration of the plan.

9. *Realistic budgets and time frames.* Realistic time frames and realistic budgets are prepared for each new product and for the entire process.

New product planning is not forced to act in a crisis mode whenever top management is pressured to "do something fast" to improve sales, profits, or the corporate persona. Budgets and time frames for new products are agreed upon by line managers and the product planning team. Deadlines and budgets are not dictated from the executive suite, but rather developed through a consensus based on the reality of each new product opportunity.

10. *Politics minimized.* A highly politicized product planning process always produces many more losers than winners. Product concepts must be judged impartially on their merits, not based upon the stature or power of the person who proposes them. Those people whose skills are more political than substantive are kept off the product planning team. This above all must be done. It has been said more in sorrow than in jest that the Walt Kelly aphorism "We have met the enemy and he is us" was invented to describe the new product planning team in the large, conservative, bureaucratized American company.

Too often people confuse the need to market winning new products and to avoid marketing the Loser new products with the rise and fall of their own careers. Everyone wants in on the sure thing. No one wants to be a product champion on the iffy product that will require everyone's best efforts to make it in the marketplace.

11. *Investment in market makeready programs.* Many new products require upfront investment in time, talent, and money to educate the market relative to the unique merits of the new product. Successful companies accept this reality and build the necessary resources into their new product planning budgets.

Market makeready funds are often the hardest to secure since they "fall between two stools." The question of whether to charge this market makeready investment against the marketing budget or the product planning budget often complicates the decision to make this important investment.

12. *Support from finance department.* Financial people view

themselves as part of the new product planning process, not as being in an adversarial role. They can exercise proper financial oversight and insist on financial discipline, but they abandon the "Dr. No" role that they are often required to assume in companies whose total focus is on the very short term.

In the winning companies that pour forth a stream of new products, a finance person is usually part of the product planning team. This individual is thus able both to explain and, where necessary, defend the budget overruns that are often inherent in the new product planning process.

Figure E-1 summarizes the twelve keys to success in bringing new products to market.

**Figure E-1.** Twelve keys to success in bringing new products to market.

# APPENDIX A

# What We Learn From the Mini-Histories

I hope you've found the mini-histories instructive, entertaining, and enlightening. Thirty-six mini-histories are, of course, too small a number to be statistically projectable to the universe of new product introductions. However, a tabulation of the outcomes of the new product introductions covered in the mini-histories by type of product and by end result does provide additional insights on the product planning process. This score card is found in Table A-1.

**Table A-1.** Score card on the Mini-Histories.

| Product Category | Big Winner | Modest Winner | Loser | Total |
|---|---|---|---|---|
| Breakthrough | 9 | 2 | 6 | 17 |
| "It's New for Us" | 2 | – | 1 | 3 |
| New, Improved, Next Generation | 6 | 3 | 3 | 12 |
| Line Extension | – | – | 1 | 1 |
| 3 Rs | 2 | – | – | 2 |
| Total | 19 | 5 | 11 | 35 * |

*Plus one "too early to tell" product.

Review of the case histories reveals several useful patterns. Breakthrough products tend to be either Big Winners or Losers. Only a minority wind up in the in-between Modest Winner category. When breakthrough products fail, they fail big and usually right away. While a small fraction, e.g., The Donvier Ice Cream Maker (see Appendix B), can be salvaged by adopting a radically different plan, in most cases the proper decision is to let it go, cut your losses, and critique what went wrong so you will do it right the next time.

This was the approach taken by IBM in disposing of the PC Junior and in terminating DiscoVision Associates, its videodisc joint venture with Pioneer and MCA. Most Big Winner break-through products are Big Winners from day one, but a minor-ity, especially high-tech products, need a prolonged period of market introduction or market makeready before they become Big Winners.

Finally, the mini-histories underline the importance of having the right people doing the right jobs as a key to success in bringing new products to market. Unfortunately, many of the standard texts on product planning could leave one with the impression that if you have the right system, with the right checkpoints and controls, success in new products will be yours.

This formulaic approach to new products looks good on paper, but it often clashes with how things work in the real world. My experience is that good people are more important than precise systems. Good people will work out the right system to get the job done. The penultimate system won't produce winning new products unless the people are the right people for the job.

If I could leave you with only one final thought, it would be this: Please devote considerable time and attention to staffing your new product planning operation with the right kinds of people, and strive for the right mix of talents for your company and your industry. Most important, make sure that this vital life support function has the proper stature in the company and the strong, clear mandate that will allow the new product planning team to devote its full time and energy to getting the job done.

# APPENDIX B

# One Company's New Product Market Introduction: The Donvier Ice Cream Maker

## Situation Analysis

The consumer ice cream maker business had been a static or declining market for a number of years prior to 1985. The principal competitors were Simac, Gaggia, and Richmond Cedar. The electric model products were efficient but high priced (often over $200) and had very limited upscale markets. The low-end products selling in the $50-plus range were mechanical, required hand-cranking and ice, and were inconvenient to use.

Nippon Light Metal Company (NLM), a major Japanese producer of aluminum products, developed an ice cream

This market introduction plan is presented for instructional purposes only. It is based on actual work performed, but the quantitative section including sales and profit data has been altered to protect client confidentiality.

maker, basically a cylindrical pot filled with Freon, that when frozen enabled the consumer to create ice cream, sherbert, or other frozen desserts in twenty minutes with only three intermittent turns of the handle.

NLM failed in an earlier attempt to introduce the product in the United States because it was unfamiliar with the U.S. market and chose to enter it through low-end discount house chains that did not merchandise or promote the product.

The product, which NLM called the Donvier Ice Cream Maker, had been very successful in Japan. After analyzing results of this first American market introduction, NLM wisely went back to the drawing board. The new market entry strategy enabled it to achieve a successful new product launch.

This new strategy called for the establishment of a working partnership with an American entrepreneur that took the form of an American marketing and distribution company called Nikkal Industries, Ltd.

## Market Analysis and Research Program

After a thorough review of alternate distribution strategies, including direct sale of the Donvier on TV via a direct response 800 number, it was decided to position the product as an upscale kitchen appliance, to be sold to young homemakers with an interest in nutrition and in creative food preparation.

The first research module was a product placement test among approximately seventy-five preselected respondents in two major markets. Affluent female homemakers with children in private nursery school and preschool were chosen to participate in this test. Each participant was given an ice cream maker with directions and asked to use it a minimum of three times over a two-week period in return for a participation fee. The results of this test were favorable beyond our expectations, with an approval rate over 80 percent.

Encouraged by this finding, the company booked space at the gourmet food trade show in San Francisco. The booth was modest and in a remote corner, but the Donvier ice cream maker was, by a wide margin, the hot new item of the show.

Orders were booked with major department stores and gourmet food outlets.

Most important, a seasoned and sophisticated sales and marketing executive with an established following of customers was retained as vice-president of sales and marketing.

Two additional market research projects were authorized to assist the company to plan its strategy for this suddenly hot new product. The first study concentrated on determining the in-depth reactions of consumers to the process of making home-made ice cream to provide guidance to the advertising agency on the proper positioning and communication strategy for the product.

This research determined that most prospects in the target market accepted on face value that home-made ice cream was better tasting and more nutritious than store-bought ice cream. The research also indicated that product acceptance would be better in Middle America than in large sophisticated markets on the East and West Coasts.

The other market research project was conducted among early purchasers of the ice cream maker, based on warranty card returns. This study, conducted via direct mail, achieved a high response rate (35 percent) and provided strong evidence that people were indeed using the product. Most important, the research indicated that Donvier owners thought that the product provided good value for the money and was not considered to be merely a fad or novelty.

## Market Rollout Program

A small creative agency, Spencer & Leichman (now the Leichman Group), was awarded the Donvier account over four other agencies.

Emboldened by the research results, an imaginative, witty television commercial was created that managed to "cut through the clutter" of the many ads competing for the viewer's attention. This television ad was supplemented by a program of print advertising in trade magazines.

There were three other key elements in the market rollout plan.

1. *A vigorous and aggressive campaign to get editorial coverage for the Donvier ice cream maker in the food and life-style columns of major newspapers.* Within one year of the market introduction, the Donvier had received over one hundred fifty editorial articles, often complete with pictures of the product in use, from newspapers and magazines throughout the country.

This kind of editorial publicity does not happen by luck or by accident. A small public relations agency with experience and contacts in this product category worked diligently to cultivate food editors at major newspapers throughout the country to orchestrate this continuing editorial coverage of this hot new product.

2. *A continuing program of in-store product demonstrations in several hundred major accounts during the first eighteen months of the product rollout.* These demonstrations were carefully planned and scripted by the marketing department and were very effective in demonstrating that the product was fun and easy to use for adults and children as well. A firm that specializes in the recruitment, training, and supervision of in-store demonstration programs was retained to manage and coordinate this element of the market rollout program.

3. *The creation of a demonstration video to supplement and ultimately to replace the use of live product demonstrations.* From research and subsequent sales experience, we learned that people did not need to taste the ice cream to be convinced to buy the Donvier ice cream maker. They merely had to be convinced that the product actually worked (and was not difficult to use). Once a critical mass of satisfied users had been created, it was determined that the switch from very expensive in-person demonstrations to cost-effective video demonstrations could be made without any negative effect on sales patterns.

## Establishment of the Organization and Infrastructure

Since Nikkal Industries, Ltd., was a startup company, it was also necessary to deal with the administrative and operational issues discussed in Chapter Twenty-Three.

Convinced that the timing was right for a major product introduction, the planning was accelerated, and within a six-month period the company was able to accomplish the following key elements necessary to the market introduction:

- Selection of a full-service warehouse in Virginia Beach, Virginia, to handle inventory and physical distribution
- The building of a staff of thirty people to manage and run a company that would grow from start-up to $10 million in annual sales in eighteen months
- The creation of a network of approximately 1,000 dealers for the product and its related items
- The building of a nationwide sales rep network and the hiring of a highly experienced marketing and sales executive from a major competitor

## Sales Forecasts

The sales forecast was made separately for the two sizes of product, the one-pint and the one-quart size. In Japan, where over one million units were sold, the pint size sold at a two-to-one ratio over the quart size. Research indicated that the reverse pattern would hold true in the United States. We reasoned that the small size of many Japanese refrigerators and freezers, rather than a demand for smaller units, was the key factor in the selection of the smaller size. This analysis proved to be correct and a timely adjustment of the purchase order helped to avoid stock-out and back-order problems during the rollout period.

| Sales Forecast—Units | | | |
|---|---|---|---|
| | _1985_ | _1986_ | _1987_ |
| Quart size | 150,000 | 300,000 | 350,000 |
| Pint size | 100,000 | 150,000 | 150,000 |
| Half-pint size | — | 50,000 | 100,000 |
| Total units | 250,000 | 500,000 | 600,000 |

## Conclusion

The company grew from startup to thirty people during a six-month period in 1985. Actual total unit sales to retailers reached the level of one million by end of 1986. The product achieved a market share in excess of 30 percent by early 1987. A nationwide sales representative network was created in a six-month period and over 1,000 accounts were established. As of the end of 1986 when our assignment was completed, the Donvier ice cream maker had become the sales leader in its product category.

## Postscript

Four million units of the Donvier Ice Cream Maker were sold in the United States through the end of 1989. Unfortunately, lack of strong administrative management and lack of cost control led to differences between Nikkal Industries, Ltd., and its Japanese partners. Rights to the Donvier line have been sold to Krups, a major German kitchen appliance firm, which plans to expand the product line and build on the brand acceptance of the Donvier ice cream maker in the 1990s.

# APPENDIX C

# Bibliography and Suggested Reading List

**Books and Booklets**

Bobrow, Edwin E., and Dennis W. Shafer. *Pioneering New Products, A Market Survival Guide.* Homewood, Ill.: Dow Jones-Irwin, 1987.

Caris-McManus, Jeannemarie. *The New Product Development Planner.* New York: AMACOM, 1991.

Cooper, Robert G. *Winning at New Products.* Reading, Mass.: Addison-Wesley, 1986.

Drucker, Peter F. *Innovation and Entrepreneurship, Practice and Principles.* New York: Harper & Row, 1985.

Freedman, George. *The Pursuit of Innovation.* New York: AMACOM, 1988.

Gruenwald, George. *New Product Development.* Lincolnwood, Ill.: NTC Business Books, 1985.

Hanan, Mack, and Peter Karp. *Customer Satisfaction: How to Maximize, Measure, and Market Your Company's "Ultimate Product."* New York: AMACOM, 1989.

Hawken, P. *Growing a Business.* New York: Simon & Schuster, 1987.

Kanter, Rosabeth Moss. *Changemasters.* New York: Simon & Schuster, 1983.

Kuczmarski, Thomas D. *Managing New Products, Competing Through Excellence.* Englewood Cliffs, N.J.: Prentice-Hall, 1988.

Levitt, Theodore. *Marketing Imagination.* New York: The Free Press, 1983.

*New Products Management for the 1980's.* New York: Booz, Allen & Hamilton, Inc., 1982.

Pascale, Richard Tanner. *Managing on the Edge.* New York: Simon & Schuster, 1990.

Pessemier, Edgar A. *Product Management, Strategy and Organization.* Melbourne, Fla.: Robert E. Krieger Publishing Company, 1976.

Peters, Thomas J., and Robert H. Waterman, Jr. *In Search of Excellence.* New York: Harper & Row, 1982.

Peters, Tom, and Nancy Austin. *A Passion for Excellence.* New York: Random House, 1985.

Poole, Thomas M. "Proven Guidelines for New Product Success." Presentation to New Products Marketing Workshops. Sponsored by the Association of National Advertisers, Inc.

Porter, M. E. *Competitive Advantage, Creating and Sustaining Superior Performance.* New York: The Free Press, 1985.

———. *Competitive Strategy, Techniques for Analyzing Industries and Competitors.* New York: The Free Press, 1980.

Ries, Al, and Jack Trout. *Positioning, The Battle for Your Mind.* New York: Warner Books, 1981.

## Articles and Newsletters

*The Donvier Story: A Case History in New Product Reintroduction* (newsletter). From The Planning Room. John Hall & Co., Inc., Vol. 3, No. 7, 1989.

"How Managers Can Succeed Through Speed." *Fortune* (February 13, 1989), pp. 54ff.

"Japan's Capital Spending Spree." *Fortune* (April 9, 1990), pp. 91ff.

Main, Jeremy. "U.S. Manufacturing Is Back." *Fortune* (May 21, 1990), pp. 55–56.

Mandell, Mel, and Brian Murphy. "Wake-Up Strategies for Tired R&D Projects." *High Technology Business* (February 1989), pp. 22ff.

Takeuchi, Hirotaka, and Ikujiro Nonaka. "The New Product Development Game." *High Technology Business* (February 1989), pp. 22ff.

"You Can Lead a Restaurateur to Perrier, But...." *Business Week* (June 25, 1990), p. 25.

# Index